Proud Wealth

BUILDING ABUNDANCE ON
YOUR OWN TERMS

Gregory True

ISBN:

Dedication

For my late husband John L. Tokos Jr. You still inspire me every day.

Contents

Preface

This book is dedicated to the resilient, vibrant, and often overlooked LGBTQ+ community. To the young people questioning their identities and navigating the complexities of adulthood; to the couples building lives together, defying societal norms and forging their own paths; to the families, chosen and biological, who offer unwavering love and support. This is for those who have faced discrimination, prejudice, and systemic barriers, yet persevere with unwavering strength and determination. This is for the activists, advocates, and allies who tirelessly fight for equality and justice. This work is a testament to your courage, your love, and your enduring spirit. It is a beacon of hope, a roadmap to financial empowerment, and a celebration of your unique and valuable contributions to the world. May this guide empower you to create financial security and build a future filled with joy, love, and abundance. May it serve as a testament to the resilience of the human spirit and the power of community. We celebrate your strength and recognize your intrinsic worth. This book is for you.

Introduction

Financial security is a fundamental pillar of well-being, yet for many in the LGBTQ+ community, achieving it presents unique and significant challenges. Systemic inequalities, discrimination, and a lack of culturally competent financial resources can create significant obstacles. This book is designed to address these challenges head-on, providing a comprehensive guide tailored to the specific needs and circumstances of LGBTQ+ individuals, couples, and families. We move beyond generic financial advice, delving into the nuances of LGBTQ+ experiences and offering tailored strategies to overcome obstacles related to housing discrimination, healthcare disparities, and the complexities of family structures that go beyond traditional norms.

Whether you are a young adult just starting to manage your finances, a couple navigating shared resources and long-term planning, or a family building a secure future for your children, this book offers practical tools and strategies for achieving financial success. We explore budgeting, debt management, investing, and estate planning, providing clear, concise information that is both informative and empathetic. Throughout the book, we highlight the importance of community support and advocacy, emphasizing the power of collective action in achieving systemic change. This is more than just a financial guide; it's an invitation to join a community committed to empowerment, resilience, and the creation of a brighter financial future for all. We emphasize a holistic approach, recognizing that financial well-being is intricately linked to emotional well-being and that past traumas can significantly impact financial decision-making. We encourage self-compassion and celebrate the strengths of the LGBTQ+ community, empowering readers to take control of their financial destiny. Together, we will navigate this journey towards financial freedom, building a more equitable and inclusive financial landscape for all.

1

BUILDING A FOUNDATION: UNDERSTANDING YOUR FINANCIAL LANDSCAPE

Assessing Your Current Financial Situation

Understanding your current financial situation is the cornerstone of building a secure financial future. This isn't about judgment; it's about empowerment. Many within the LGBTQ+ community face unique financial challenges stemming from systemic discrimination, historical inequalities, and sometimes, past trauma. This section provides a safe and supportive space to honestly assess your finances, without shame or judgment, and to begin building a plan for a brighter financial future.

The first step is creating a detailed budget. A budget isn't about restriction; it's about clarity. It's a tool to understand where your money is going and identify areas where you can make adjustments to achieve your financial goals. There are many methods to approach budgeting. Some prefer the 50/30/20 rule, allocating 50% of your income to needs, 30% to wants, and 20% to savings and debt repayment. Others find success with zero-based budgeting, where every dollar is assigned a purpose. The best method is the one that works best for you and your lifestyle.

To create your budget, start by gathering your financial records for the past three months. This includes bank statements, credit card statements, pay stubs, and any other documentation related to your income and expenses. Carefully categorize your expenses. Separate needs (housing, utilities, food, transportation) from wants (entertainment, dining out, subscriptions). Be as detailed as possible. Often, small, seemingly insignificant expenses accumulate quickly. That daily latte, the subscription boxes you rarely use, those impulse online purchases – these all add up over time.

Many free budgeting apps can streamline this process. Mint, Personal Capital, and YNAB (You Need A Budget) are just a few examples. These apps automatically categorize transactions, track your spending, and offer helpful visualizations of your finances. They also often provide features like goal setting and budgeting tools which can help you stay focused on the big picture. If technology isn't your thing, a simple spreadsheet or even a notebook and pen will work just as well. The key is consistency. Track your expenses regularly – daily or weekly – to ensure accuracy and gain a clear picture of your spending habits.

Once you have a clear picture of your income and expenses, you can identify areas for potential savings. Are there recurring subscriptions you can cancel or downgrade? Can you reduce your spending on groceries by meal planning or cooking at home more often? Can you find more affordable options for transportation, entertainment, or other expenses? Remember, small changes can have a significant impact over time. For example, reducing your daily coffee expenditure by just $5 can save you over $1,800 a year.

This process of assessing your current financial situation requires honesty and self-compassion. Many LGBTQ+ individuals have experienced financial instability due to discrimination, job loss, or unexpected medical expenses, particularly those related to gender-affirming care, which is often under- or uninsured. Recognizing the impact of these factors is crucial. Avoid self-blame or judgment; focus on building a plan for a more secure future.

Remember that your financial situation is not static; it's dynamic and will evolve over time. Regularly reviewing and adjusting your budget is crucial to ensure it aligns with your goals and changing circumstances. Consider scheduling a monthly review of your budget to monitor your spending and make necessary adjustments. This ongoing process allows for flexibility and helps prevent unexpected financial surprises.

Beyond creating a budget, understanding your assets and liabilities is equally important. Assets are what you own – bank accounts, investments, property, vehicles. Liabilities are what you owe – credit card debt, student loans, mortgages. Listing all your assets and liabilities will give you a snapshot of your net worth (assets minus liabilities). Tracking this net worth over time can be a powerful motivator and provide a tangible measure of your financial progress.

For many in the LGBTQ+ community, building wealth may have been particularly challenging due to historical and ongoing discrimination in employment, housing, and access to financial services. It's important to acknowledge these systemic barriers and to approach financial planning with understanding and self-compassion.

For example, the cost of gender-affirming healthcare can be substantial, often placing a significant financial strain on transgender and gender non-conforming individuals. Many insurance plans don't fully cover these costs. This can lead to significant medical debt, compounding the financial challenges already faced. If you're struggling with medical debt, exploring options like negotiating with providers, debt consolidation, or seeking financial assistance programs is crucial. There are numerous organizations dedicated to supporting the LGBTQ+ community that can offer guidance and resources.

Another common challenge is facing discrimination in employment, leading to lower earning potential or difficulty securing stable employment. This can make saving and investing more difficult. If you've faced discrimination, consider seeking legal counsel to understand your rights and explore potential recourse.

Navigating housing insecurity is another significant issue impacting the financial well-being of LGBTQ+ individuals.

Discrimination in housing can lead to difficulty finding safe and affordable housing, resulting in higher housing costs and financial instability. If you suspect you've experienced housing discrimination, report it to the appropriate authorities and seek assistance from organizations dedicated to fair housing practices.

In addition to tracking income and expenses, understanding your cash flow is vital. Cash flow is the difference between your income and your expenses. A positive cash flow means you have more money coming in than going out, while a negative cash flow means the opposite. A negative cash flow can lead to debt accumulation, which puts a strain on your ability to save and invest. If you're experiencing negative cash flow, it's essential to identify the cause and develop strategies to improve it, such as increasing your income or reducing your expenses.

This process of assessing your financial situation may uncover some uncomfortable truths. It may reveal areas where you've been overspending or where debt has accumulated. Remember, this isn't a sign of failure; it's an opportunity for growth and change. By acknowledging your current situation honestly, you can create a plan to improve your financial well-being.

Taking the time to complete a thorough assessment of your current financial situation is a significant step towards securing your financial future. Remember, building financial stability takes time and effort, and it's a journey, not a destination. By taking these steps and continuously reviewing your progress, you can build a solid foundation for a more secure and prosperous future. Embrace this process, celebrate your successes, and don't hesitate to seek support and guidance along the way. The resources and support networks within the LGBTQ+ community are vast and readily available. You are not alone in this journey.

Addressing Debt and Creating A Debt Reduction Plan

Addressing debt can feel daunting, especially when considering the unique financial hurdles many in the LGBTQ+ community face. However, understanding the different types of debt and developing a strategic repayment plan is crucial for building a secure financial future. This isn't about shame or self-blame; it's about empowerment and taking control of your financial narrative.

Let's begin by categorizing debt. We commonly encounter several types:

Credit Card Debt: This is often high-interest debt, accruing interest charges daily. The high interest rates can quickly snowball your debt, making repayment a challenging uphill battle. Mindful spending habits and promptly paying off balances in full each month are crucial to avoiding this trap.

Student Loan Debt: For many, student loans represent a significant investment in their future. However, the repayment process can be complex, with various repayment plans and potential for forgiveness programs available. Understanding your loan terms, exploring repayment options, and proactively engaging with your loan servicer are vital steps in managing this debt effectively. For LGBTQ+ individuals, educational expenses can be exacerbated by potential discrimination in scholarships or financial aid. Advocating for more inclusive financial aid policies is an essential step towards equitable access to education.

Medical Debt: This is an especially prevalent concern for the LGBTQ+ community, particularly for transgender and gender non-conforming individuals undergoing gender- affirming care. The cost of such care can be substantial, often exceeding what insurance covers. This can lead to significant medical debt which requires careful attention. Advocating for comprehensive insurance coverage for gender-affirming care is paramount, but in the meantime, exploring options like negotiating payment plans with providers, seeking financial assistance from LGBTQ+ organizations, or considering medical debt relief programs is essential.

Personal Loans: These loans are taken out for various purposes, often with fixed repayment schedules and interest rates. While they can be helpful for managing unexpected expenses or consolidating debt, it's crucial to carefully compare interest rates and terms before borrowing. Avoid predatory lenders who target vulnerable communities with high-interest loans and unfavorable terms. Be wary of loans with hidden fees or overly complex terms.

Mortgages: For many, owning a home represents a significant financial achievement. However, mortgages represent a large, long-term debt obligation. Understanding mortgage terms, including interest rates, repayment schedules, and potential risks, is essential for responsible homeownership. Within the LGBTQ+ community, accessing fair and equitable housing can present challenges due to historical and ongoing discrimination. Organizations working to combat housing discrimination offer invaluable support and resources in navigating this complex landscape.

Once you've identified the types and amounts of your debt,

you can start creating a debt reduction plan. Several strategies can be effective:

The Debt Snowball Method: This method focuses on paying off the smallest debt first, regardless of interest rate. This provides a sense of accomplishment and momentum, motivating you to continue tackling larger debts. The psychological boost can be incredibly powerful.

The Debt Avalanche Method: This strategy prioritizes paying off debts with the highest interest rates first, minimizing the overall interest paid over time. While this might not be as emotionally satisfying initially, it can result in significant long-term savings.

Debt Consolidation: This involves combining multiple debts into a single loan, often with a lower interest rate. This simplifies repayment, providing a more manageable monthly payment. However, carefully review the terms of the consolidation loan to ensure it's a genuinely beneficial option. Avoid predatory lenders who might offer seemingly attractive rates but then include high fees or unfavorable terms.

Negotiating with Creditors: It is possible to negotiate with creditors to reduce the amount you owe or to establish a more manageable repayment plan. Many are willing to work with borrowers facing financial difficulties. However, approaching this negotiation with clear and concise communication is crucial. Documenting all communication is also essential.

Seeking Professional Help: Credit counseling agencies can provide guidance and support in developing a debt management plan. They can help you negotiate with creditors and create a budget to help you stay on track. These agencies can be invaluable resources, especially when navigating complex financial situations.

Building a debt reduction plan requires careful consideration of your individual circumstances. For many in the LGBTQ+ community, additional factors, such as discrimination in employment or access to healthcare, can significantly impact debt management. Recognizing these challenges and adapting your plan accordingly is crucial.

For example, a transgender individual facing high medical debt due to gender-affirming care might need to prioritize this debt over other forms of debt, while simultaneously seeking financial assistance from organizations specializing in LGBTQ+ healthcare access. A same-sex couple navigating discrimination in housing might need to adjust their debt repayment plan to account for unexpectedly high housing costs. Acknowledging these unique circumstances and building a flexible, adaptable plan is essential for success.

Creating a realistic budget is inseparable from debt

reduction. Track your income and expenses meticulously, identifying areas where you can cut back. Even small reductions in spending can accumulate significant savings over time. Prioritize essential expenses such as housing, food, and transportation, and carefully evaluate discretionary spending. Explore affordable alternatives for entertainment, transportation, and other non-essential items. Consider using budgeting apps or spreadsheets to track your progress and monitor your spending habits.

Remember, tackling debt is a marathon, not a sprint. There will be setbacks and challenges along the way. It's important to be patient with yourself, celebrate your progress, and seek support when needed. The LGBTQ+ community has a vast network of organizations and resources dedicated to providing financial guidance and support. Don't hesitate to reach out for assistance; you are not alone on this journey towards financial freedom. By developing a comprehensive debt reduction plan, actively managing your finances, and seeking support when necessary, you can create a more secure and financially stable future. This is a testament to your strength and resilience, and a foundation upon which you can build a prosperous future. Remember to celebrate small victories along the way; the journey towards financial wellbeing is as significant as the destination itself.

Understanding Credit Scores And Building Good Credit

Understanding your credit score is paramount to achieving financial well-being. It's a three-digit number that acts as a snapshot of your creditworthiness, reflecting how reliably you've managed your credit in the past. Lenders use this score to assess the risk involved in lending you money – whether it's for a credit card, a loan, or a mortgage. A higher credit score typically translates to better interest rates and more favorable loan terms, saving you significant money over time. Conversely, a low credit score can severely limit your access to credit and lead to higher interest rates, making it harder to achieve your financial goals.

The most commonly used credit scoring models are FICO and VantageScore. While the specific calculations differ slightly, both scores range from 300 to 850, with higher scores indicating better credit.

Many factors contribute to your credit score, but some key elements include:

Payment History (35%): This is the most significant factor. Consistently paying your bills on time is crucial. Even one missed payment can negatively impact your score, and multiple late payments can significantly lower it. Set up automatic payments to avoid accidental late payments. Consider using budgeting apps or calendar reminders to stay on top of due dates.

Amounts Owed (30%): This refers to your credit utilization ratio – the amount of credit you're using compared to your total available credit. Keeping your credit utilization low (ideally below 30%) is essential. For example, if you have a credit card with a $1,000 limit, it's best to keep your balance below $300. High credit utilization suggests you are heavily reliant on credit, increasing the perceived risk to lenders.

Length of Credit History (15%): Lenders like to see a long and consistent history of responsible credit use. The longer your credit accounts have been open, the better your score will likely be. Avoid closing old accounts unless absolutely necessary, as this can shorten your credit history.

New Credit (10%): Opening many new credit accounts in a short period can negatively affect your score, as it signals increased risk. Only apply for credit when you genuinely need it, and avoid applying for multiple accounts simultaneously.

Credit Mix (10%): Having a variety of credit accounts (e.g., credit cards, installment loans, mortgages) demonstrates your ability to manage different types of credit responsibly. However, don't open accounts just to diversify your credit mix; focus on responsible use of the accounts you already have.

For the LGBTQ+ community, building and maintaining

good credit can present unique challenges. Historical and ongoing discrimination can impact employment stability, income levels, and access to financial resources, all of which can affect creditworthiness. For instance, transgender individuals may face employment discrimination, leading to income instability and difficulty in managing credit accounts. Same-sex couples may encounter challenges in accessing joint credit accounts or mortgages due to discriminatory lending practices.

These systemic barriers highlight the need for proactive strategies to build and maintain good credit. This might involve seeking support from LGBTQ+-affirming financial institutions or credit counselors who understand the unique challenges faced by this community. These organizations can provide personalized guidance, helping individuals navigate the complexities of credit building while accounting for unique circumstances. For example, a credit counselor might help a transgender individual develop a budget to manage medical debt related to gender-affirming care, ensuring that their payment history remains positive despite high medical expenses.

Actively monitoring your credit reports is crucial. You are entitled to a free credit report from each of the three major credit bureaus – Equifax, Experian, and TransUnion – annually through AnnualCreditReport.com. Regularly reviewing your reports helps identify errors or fraudulent activity that could negatively impact your score. Dispute any inaccuracies immediately with the respective credit bureau. This vigilance can save you from significant financial distress in the long run.

If you've discovered errors on your credit report or are struggling to improve your credit score, consider seeking professional help from a reputable credit repair service. However, be cautious and choose carefully. Research the company thoroughly, ensuring it's legitimate and avoiding those promising unrealistic results or charging excessive fees upfront. Many reputable services work with you to dispute inaccuracies, develop a plan to address negative information, and provide financial education. The cost of these services should be weighed against the potential long-term benefits of a better credit score.

Building good credit is a continuous process. It requires discipline, vigilance, and a proactive approach. However, the rewards are substantial. A good credit score opens doors to better financial opportunities, allowing you to access lower interest rates on loans, secure more favorable terms on credit cards, and even potentially qualify for better insurance rates. For the LGBTQ+ community, achieving financial stability can be especially empowering, mitigating the impact of systemic barriers and creating a more secure future. Remember, your financial well-being is essential, and building good credit is a significant step toward achieving it. It's a journey that requires patience, persistence, and the support of trustworthy resources. Don't hesitate to seek assistance; you are not alone in this endeavor. By focusing on responsible credit management and actively monitoring your credit reports, you can establish a strong financial foundation that will serve you well for years to come. The journey towards financial security is an investment in your future self, and a testament to your resilience and determination. Celebrate each milestone; even small achievements are significant steps in building your financial independence.

Emergency Fund Essentials for LGBTQ Individuals

Building a robust emergency fund is not merely a suggestion; it's a crucial cornerstone of financial security, especially for members of the LGBTQ+ community. This demographic often faces unique financial vulnerabilities that necessitate a more proactive and comprehensive approach to savings. While everyone benefits from having a financial safety net, the necessity is heightened for LGBTQ+ individuals who may experience higher rates of discrimination in employment, housing, and healthcare, leading to increased financial instability.

Consider the scenario of a transgender individual undergoing gender-affirming care. The cost of medical procedures, hormone therapy, and related services can be substantial, potentially placing a significant strain on even the most carefully managed budget. A sudden job loss or unexpected medical complication could easily lead to overwhelming debt if an emergency fund isn't in place. Similarly, same-sex couples may encounter challenges securing affordable housing or facing discriminatory practices in the mortgage market, creating further vulnerability to financial shocks. These situations highlight the critical need for a substantial emergency fund that can act as a buffer against unforeseen circumstances.

The recommended amount for an emergency fund is generally three to six months' worth of living expenses. However, for LGBTQ+ individuals facing potential systemic discrimination, this figure might need to be higher – perhaps even exceeding six months. The additional cushion provides a vital safety net to navigate periods of unemployment, unexpected medical bills, or other financial hardships. Calculating your living expenses requires a realistic assessment of all regular monthly costs, including rent or mortgage payments, utilities, groceries, transportation, insurance premiums, debt payments, and any other recurring expenses. Be sure to factor in potential fluctuations and increase the estimate to account for those possibilities.

Building an emergency fund requires discipline and prioritization. It's essential to develop a realistic budget, track your spending, and identify areas where expenses can be reduced. Even small, consistent savings add up over time. Consider automating your savings by setting up regular transfers from your checking account to your savings account. This helps ensure that saving becomes a habitual part of your financial routine, rather than an afterthought. Many financial institutions offer features like round-up programs, which automatically round up purchases to the nearest dollar and transfer the difference to your savings account. These small contributions, while individually insignificant, collectively make a substantial difference over time.

Finding the right savings vehicle is crucial. High-yield savings accounts offer a better return on your savings compared to standard savings accounts, helping your money grow while remaining readily accessible. However, it’s important to balance yield with accessibility. While certificates of deposit (CDs) often offer higher interest rates, they lock your money away for a specified period, which might not be ideal for an emergency fund. The goal is liquidity – the ability to access your funds quickly and easily when unexpected expenses arise.

Beyond the monetary aspects, building an emergency fund requires a strong mental game. It's easy to become discouraged when progress feels slow, particularly when facing financial challenges. Therefore, celebrate every milestone along the way. Acknowledge your commitment to building financial security, and remember that each small step is progress. Set realistic, achievable goals and regularly track your progress to maintain motivation.

Furthermore, remember that building an emergency fund is not a solitary endeavor. It's essential to create a supportive network, both personally and professionally. Connecting with LGBTQ+-affirming financial advisors can provide invaluable guidance tailored to the unique financial challenges faced by the community. These advisors understand the specific barriers and complexities that LGBTQ+ individuals encounter and can offer tailored financial advice to navigate them effectively. They can help with budgeting, developing a savings plan, exploring debt management strategies, and selecting appropriate investment vehicles.

Equally important is leveraging available resources and support networks within the LGBTQ+ community. Many organizations offer financial literacy workshops, credit counseling services, and other programs specifically designed to support community members. These resources offer invaluable support, knowledge sharing, and empowerment, helping individuals build confidence in managing their finances. Don't hesitate to seek support when needed. Connecting with individuals who understand your unique situation can significantly impact your financial journey.

In addition to the emotional support, the LGBTQ+ community offers strength in numbers. Sharing experiences, resources, and strategies can empower everyone involved and demonstrate the shared experience of navigating financial challenges. Remember that you are not alone in this journey; your experiences and challenges are understood and shared within a supportive network. Leveraging this collective experience and wisdom can significantly enhance your capacity to build financial resilience.

Beyond seeking professional support, consider diversifying your income streams if possible. Part-time work, freelance projects, or rental income can augment your primary income and bolster your ability to contribute to your emergency fund. Remember that financial security is a marathon, not a sprint. While progress might seem slow at times, consistent effort and the utilization of available resources will lead to a more secure and stable financial future.

While building an emergency fund is a crucial step toward financial well-being, it's not the only one. It's essential to combine it with a comprehensive financial plan that considers long-term goals such as retirement planning, investing, and estate planning. A holistic approach that incorporates all aspects of financial management is key to achieving lasting financial security and reducing financial vulnerability. Building your emergency fund is an empowering step toward achieving financial independence, giving you the ability to weather unexpected life events and pursue your goals with greater confidence and security. This financial stability allows you to focus on other aspects of your well-being, knowing that a robust financial safety net is in place to support you.

Remember that building financial resilience is not just about accumulating money; it's also about cultivating the mindset and habits that support long- term financial well-being.

Financial Self - Care And Mental Wellbeing

The journey toward financial security is inextricably linked to our mental and emotional well-being. For members of the LGBTQ+ community, this connection is particularly profound. Many individuals within this demographic have experienced discrimination, marginalization, and potentially past trauma that can significantly impact their financial decision-making, self-esteem, and overall mental health. Understanding this intricate relationship is crucial for building a solid foundation of financial resilience.

Financial stress, often stemming from precarious employment situations, housing instability, or the high cost of healthcare (especially for transgender individuals undergoing gender-affirming care), can exacerbate existing mental health concerns or trigger new ones. The constant worry about money, the fear of not being able to meet basic needs, or the shame associated with financial hardship can lead to anxiety, depression, and feelings of hopelessness. This cycle of financial instability and mental health struggles can be difficult to break, creating a vicious feedback loop that requires a multi-faceted approach to overcome.

Recognizing the impact of past trauma on current financial

behaviors is a critical first step. Many LGBTQ+ individuals have experienced discrimination and rejection, which may have instilled ingrained beliefs about their worthiness and ability to achieve financial success. These negative beliefs can manifest as avoidance behaviors, such as procrastination in addressing financial matters or a reluctance to seek professional financial help. Addressing these underlying issues is often crucial for effectively engaging with financial planning and building a secure future. Therapy, support groups, or counseling can play a significant role in this process, helping individuals process past trauma and develop healthier coping mechanisms.

Self-care practices are vital for managing the stress associated with financial challenges. While building an emergency fund provides a crucial safety net, it's equally important to prioritize activities that nurture mental and emotional well- being. This might involve engaging in regular exercise, mindfulness practices (like meditation or yoga), spending time in nature, engaging in hobbies, or pursuing creative outlets. These activities offer a much-needed counterbalance to the demands of financial planning and provide a sense of calm and stability amidst the uncertainty.

Building a strong support network is another critical component of financial self-care. Surrounding yourself with supportive friends, family members, or community members can provide emotional sustenance and practical assistance during challenging times. Sharing your experiences with trusted individuals can alleviate feelings of isolation and shame, creating a space for vulnerability and mutual understanding. The LGBTQ+ community, in particular, offers a unique source of strength and resilience, with many organizations and support groups providing a safe and welcoming environment for sharing financial concerns and seeking advice.

Learning to effectively manage stress is a crucial skill in navigating the financial landscape. Stress management techniques, such as deep breathing exercises, progressive muscle relaxation, or cognitive behavioral therapy (CBT), can help reduce anxiety and improve overall mental well- being. CBT, in particular, can be highly effective in challenging negative thought patterns and developing more adaptive coping mechanisms for handling financial setbacks. Consider working with a therapist specializing in trauma-informed care to address past experiences and develop healthy strategies for managing stress.

It's important to remember that financial planning is not a solitary endeavor. Seeking professional help from a financial advisor specializing in LGBTQ+ issues is highly recommended. These advisors possess a deep understanding of the specific financial challenges faced by the community, including the impact of discrimination and systemic inequalities. They can offer tailored advice and support in developing a comprehensive financial plan that addresses your unique circumstances and goals.

Developing a realistic budget and tracking expenses are fundamental steps towards achieving financial stability. However, it's equally crucial to approach budgeting with compassion and self-compassion. Avoid setting unrealistic goals or engaging in self-criticism if you experience setbacks. Instead, focus on celebrating small victories and acknowledging the progress you've made. Remember that building financial resilience is a marathon, not a sprint, and setbacks are a normal part of the journey.

Financial literacy is another critical factor in achieving financial wellness. Understanding basic financial concepts, such as budgeting, saving, investing, and debt management, is essential for making informed financial decisions. Numerous resources are available to enhance financial literacy, including online courses, workshops, and books specifically tailored to the LGBTQ+ community. These resources can empower individuals with the knowledge and confidence to navigate their financial lives with greater ease.

Beyond financial literacy, cultivating a positive mindset towards money is crucial. Developing a healthy relationship with money involves reframing negative beliefs and self- limiting thoughts. This may require challenging ingrained beliefs about money, recognizing personal values and goals, and cultivating a sense of abundance rather than scarcity. Working with a therapist or financial coach can provide invaluable support in this process.

The intersection of mental health and financial well-being is a complex one, particularly within the LGBTQ+ community. Addressing the unique challenges faced by this demographic requires a multifaceted approach that integrates financial planning with self-care practices, mental health support, and access to tailored resources. By embracing a holistic approach that prioritizes both financial security and emotional well-being, LGBTQ+ individuals can build a strong foundation for a more secure and fulfilling future. Remember that seeking help is a sign of strength, not weakness. Leveraging available support systems and resources empowers you to build financial resilience while nurturing your overall mental and emotional well-being. This integrated approach is key to achieving lasting financial stability and thriving in all aspects of life.

Furthermore, remember that societal expectations and pressures can also influence financial stress. The pressure to achieve specific financial milestones, conform to societal norms, or maintain a particular lifestyle can be overwhelming. Resisting these societal pressures and focusing on your individual needs and financial reality is crucial for reducing financial stress and prioritizing your mental well- being. Learning to say "no" to unnecessary expenses or commitments can free up resources and reduce financial strain.

Financial setbacks, such as job loss, unexpected medical bills, or relationship difficulties, are a normal part of life. Developing resilience in the face of adversity is vital for maintaining financial and emotional well-being. This includes building a strong support network, practicing self- compassion, and utilizing available resources to overcome challenges. Remember that you are not alone in your struggles and seeking help is a sign of strength.

Building financial resilience is a long-term process requiring patience, perseverance, and self-compassion. Celebrate every milestone along the way, no matter how small. Acknowledge your commitment to building a secure financial future, and remember that each step forward contributes to your overall well-being. By integrating financial planning with mental health support and self-care practices, you can create a more balanced and fulfilling life. Financial security is not just about accumulating wealth; it is also about cultivating a mindset and lifestyle that support your overall well-being. This holistic approach will allow you to navigate life's challenges with greater confidence, resilience, and peace of mind.

2

NAVIGATING THE LEGAL LANDSCAPE: PROTECTING YOUR ASSETS

Estate Planning for Lgbt Q Individuals And Families

Estate planning for LGBTQ+ individuals and families often presents unique challenges not encountered by heterosexual couples with traditional family structures. The absence of legal recognition in some jurisdictions, the complexities of chosen families, and the potential for discrimination necessitate a proactive and comprehensive approach to ensure assets are distributed according to one's wishes and protect loved ones. This section will explore the key elements of estate planning specifically tailored to the needs of the LGBTQ+ community.

The cornerstone of any estate plan is the will. A will dictates how your assets will be distributed after your death. For LGBTQ+ individuals, this is especially crucial. In the absence of a will, state intestacy laws will determine the distribution of your assets, and these laws may not recognize same-sex spouses or partners, leaving your chosen family and loved ones without legal recourse. A well-drafted will explicitly names your beneficiaries, ensuring your assets are distributed according to your wishes, regardless of your marital status or family structure. This includes not just financial assets, but also personal possessions and real estate. It is vital to regularly review and update your will to reflect any changes in your relationships, assets, or wishes. The importance of consulting with an estate planning attorney experienced in LGBTQ+ issues cannot be overstated. They can guide you through the complexities of state laws and ensure your will is legally sound and reflects your intentions accurately.

Beyond a will, trusts offer another powerful tool for estate planning. Trusts are legal entities that hold assets for the benefit of beneficiaries. Several types of trusts can be advantageous for LGBTQ+ individuals. For example, a revocable living trust allows you to manage your assets during your lifetime and dictate how they'll be distributed after your death, offering greater control and flexibility than a will alone. An irrevocable trust, while offering tax advantages, relinquishes control over the assets, so careful consideration is needed before establishing one. For couples who wish to protect their assets from potential creditors or future divorces, specific trust structures can be incredibly valuable. Additionally, trusts provide a mechanism to protect vulnerable beneficiaries, such as disabled individuals or those prone to financial mismanagement. They offer a structured way to ensure their long-term financial security while avoiding probate. Careful planning with legal counsel is crucial to choose the appropriate type of trust for your specific circumstances.

Powers of attorney are another critical aspect of estate planning, granting someone you trust the authority to manage your financial and legal affairs should you become incapacitated. This is essential for maintaining control over your life and assets even if you can no longer make decisions independently. Choosing the right person for this role is vital, preferably someone you trust implicitly and who understands your financial situation and wishes. A durable power of attorney remains effective even after you become incapacitated, whereas a non-durable power of attorney terminates if you lose the capacity to make decisions. It's crucial to choose the durable option to ensure continuity of care and management of your affairs. In addition to financial matters, consider establishing a healthcare power of attorney, which allows a designated person to make healthcare decisions on your behalf if you're unable to.

Healthcare directives, such as living wills and advance directives, are crucial documents that express your wishes regarding medical treatment in the event of a terminal illness or incapacitation. These documents provide peace of mind, ensuring your healthcare preferences are followed, and preventing unwanted medical interventions. Given the potential for bias or misunderstanding in the healthcare system, it's crucial for LGBTQ+ individuals to clearly articulate their wishes in these documents and designate a healthcare proxy who understands and respects their values and preferences. These documents should be specific and unambiguous, detailing your wishes regarding life-sustaining treatments, pain management, and end-of-life care.

The concept of chosen family holds particular significance within the LGBTQ+ community. These individuals— friends, partners, or chosen relatives—often play a vital role in an individual's life and should be included in estate planning documents. While legal recognition of chosen family varies by jurisdiction, incorporating them into wills, trusts, and other legal documents ensures they are appropriately provided for and their relationship with the individual is legally recognized to the extent possible. This might involve designating them as beneficiaries or guardians for children or other dependents. The inclusion of chosen family acknowledges the deeply significant relationships and bonds that define many LGBTQ+ lives and assures their financial security and well-being. Open communication with chosen family members about estate planning ensures their understanding and prevents potential disputes.

For same-sex couples, estate planning presents specific legal complexities that vary depending on the jurisdiction. In regions where same-sex marriage is legally recognized, estate planning follows a similar path to heterosexual couples. However, even in these regions, careful consideration should be given to asset protection strategies and avoiding unintended consequences due to potential legal challenges or changes in legislation. In jurisdictions where same-sex marriage is not recognized, the situation becomes significantly more complicated, requiring strategies to legally protect the assets and rights of the partner. This might involve the use of specific trust structures, joint ownership agreements, or other legal tools to achieve the desired distribution of assets. In any case, consulting with an attorney familiar with the complexities of LGBTQ+ estate planning is paramount.

The process of estate planning is not a one-time event; it's an ongoing process that should be reviewed and updated regularly. Life circumstances change – relationships evolve, assets are acquired or sold, and personal wishes may shift over time. Regular review ensures your estate plan remains relevant and accurately reflects your current situation and intentions. Significant life events, such as marriage, birth of a child, changes in health, or financial adjustments, should trigger a review and potential update of your estate plan. This proactive approach protects your assets and ensures your wishes are carried out effectively and efficiently, especially considering the ever-evolving legal landscape related to LGBTQ+ rights.

Digital assets, such as online accounts, social media profiles, and digital content, also require consideration in modern estate planning. These assets may hold significant sentimental or monetary value, and establishing clear guidelines for their management and distribution after death is crucial. This might involve designating a digital executor or creating specific instructions within a will or trust regarding access and control of these digital assets. Ignoring digital assets in estate planning leaves a gap in the overall plan and can lead to complications for your heirs.

In conclusion, estate planning for LGBTQ+ individuals and families requires a multifaceted and comprehensive approach that takes into account the unique challenges and opportunities presented by this demographic. By proactively engaging in estate planning, utilizing appropriate legal tools such as wills, trusts, and powers of attorney, and including chosen family in the process, LGBTQ+ individuals can protect their assets, provide for their loved ones, and ensure their wishes are respected. Consulting with a knowledgeable and experienced LGBTQ+-affirming attorney is vital to navigate the complexities of the legal landscape and create a robust and tailored estate plan that secures a more secure and fulfilling future for you and your loved ones. This proactive planning allows for peace of mind, knowing that your assets and relationships are protected, regardless of changing societal norms or legal complexities.

Understanding LGBTQ Inclusive Healthcare and Insurance

Understanding access to quality healthcare is paramount for everyone, but the LGBTQ+ community often faces unique and significant hurdles. These challenges are multifaceted, stemming from systemic discrimination, lack of provider knowledge and sensitivity, and the often prohibitive costs associated with healthcare, particularly for transgender and gender non-conforming individuals. Navigating the healthcare system and securing appropriate insurance coverage requires proactive planning and a thorough understanding of available resources and strategies.

One of the most immediate concerns is finding healthcare providers who are both competent and affirming. Many LGBTQ+ individuals have experienced discrimination or a lack of understanding from healthcare professionals, leading to feelings of discomfort, distrust, and ultimately, avoidance of necessary care. This is particularly true for transgender and gender non-conforming individuals who may face misgendering, invalidating their identities, and receiving inadequate or inappropriate care. Therefore, seeking out providers with demonstrated experience and expertise in working with the LGBTQ+ community is crucial. Organizations like the Human Rights Campaign (HRC) and GLAAD often maintain lists of LGBTQ+-inclusive healthcare providers, and online directories can also help in finding affirming healthcare professionals.

Beyond finding a supportive provider, access to affordable healthcare is often a major obstacle. The high cost of medical care, coupled with the complexities of insurance coverage, can deter many LGBTQ+ individuals from seeking essential medical services. This is exacerbated by the fact that some insurance plans may not adequately cover medically necessary care for transgender and gender non- conforming individuals, such as hormone replacement therapy (HRT), gender-affirming surgeries, and mental health services addressing gender dysphoria.

Insurance coverage for medically necessary care related to gender transition is a complex area. While the Affordable Care Act (ACA) prohibits discrimination based on gender identity in health insurance, the application of this protection varies across states and insurance providers. Many insurance companies still place restrictions on coverage for gender-affirming care, requiring pre-authorization, limiting the number of covered procedures, or excluding certain types of services entirely. This inconsistency necessitates a careful examination of individual insurance policies and a proactive approach to understanding the extent of coverage available.

Negotiating with insurance companies can be a challenging but potentially rewarding process. Many individuals have found success by meticulously documenting their medical need for specific procedures or treatments, obtaining letters of medical necessity from their physicians, and appealing denials through the appropriate channels. Understanding the appeals process within one's insurance plan is crucial, and seeking assistance from patient advocacy groups can

significantly improve the chances of successful negotiation. These groups offer expertise in navigating the complexities of insurance claims and appeals, often providing free or low- cost assistance to individuals facing challenges in obtaining necessary care.

Preventive care is just as crucial for LGBTQ+ individuals as it is for anyone else, but systemic barriers and fear of discrimination can lead to underutilization of these services. Regular check-ups, screenings for sexually transmitted infections (STIs), and mental health support are all essential components of preventative care. However, negative experiences with the healthcare system may cause some individuals to avoid routine check-ups, leading to potential health risks. Therefore, finding providers who foster a safe and inclusive environment is vital in encouraging regular preventative care.

The unique healthcare needs of transgender and gender non-conforming individuals require particular attention. Access to HRT, gender-affirming surgeries, and mental health services addressing gender dysphoria is often critical for their overall well-being. The cost of these services can be

substantial, and obtaining adequate insurance coverage can be particularly difficult. As discussed earlier, this necessitates a proactive approach to navigating insurance policies, appealing denials, and seeking assistance from advocacy groups.

Furthermore, mental health services are crucial for the LGBTQ+ community, which faces higher rates of anxiety, depression, and other mental health conditions due to societal stigma, discrimination, and other stressors. Finding mental health professionals who are knowledgeable about and affirming of LGBTQ+ identities is vital in ensuring that individuals receive appropriate and effective care. Therapy can play a significant role in supporting individuals throughout their journeys, providing a safe space to process experiences of discrimination and navigate challenges related to identity and self-expression.

Access to mental healthcare is often hindered by financial constraints and limited availability of culturally competent providers. Many individuals face long waiting lists and high costs for therapy, making it inaccessible to many. Exploring options like community mental health clinics, sliding-scale therapy, and telehealth services can expand access to mental health care for those facing financial limitations.

Support resources are available to assist LGBTQ+ individuals in navigating the complexities of healthcare and insurance. Many organizations offer assistance with insurance claims, provider referrals, and advocacy in accessing necessary care. These organizations often have expertise in navigating the specific challenges faced by the LGBTQ+ community and can provide invaluable support to those facing obstacles in obtaining adequate healthcare. Utilizing these resources is highly recommended, particularly when dealing with insurance disputes or navigating the complexities of gender-affirming care.

The financial aspect of healthcare is intricately intertwined with access to care. Understanding insurance policies, negotiating with insurance companies, and accessing affordable healthcare options are all critical factors in ensuring that LGBTQ+ individuals have access to the medical services they need. Proactive planning, combined with the utilization of available support resources, can significantly improve the likelihood of obtaining quality and affirming healthcare. The ongoing fight for LGBTQ+ equality includes advocating for policies that ensure equitable access to healthcare for all, regardless of sexual orientation or gender identity. This requires continued engagement with advocacy groups and elected officials to promote policies that ensure access to comprehensive and affordable healthcare for the entire LGBTQ+ community. Ultimately, the pursuit of healthcare equity is a vital component of ensuring a more just and equitable society for all.

Legal Protections Against Discrimination

The fight for equality extends beyond healthcare access; it encompasses securing legal protections against discrimination in various aspects of life. The LGBTQ+ community faces unique challenges in navigating legal systems often designed without their lived experiences in mind. Understanding your rights and knowing where to seek recourse when discrimination occurs is crucial to protecting your assets and well-being.

One of the most significant areas where legal protection is vital is housing. Fair Housing laws, both at the federal and state levels, prohibit discrimination based on sexual orientation and gender identity. The Fair Housing Act of 1968, as amended, explicitly prohibits discrimination in housing based on race, color, national origin, religion, sex, familial status, and disability. Crucially, many states and municipalities have expanded this protection to include sexual orientation and gender identity, making it illegal for landlords to refuse to rent to, evict, or otherwise discriminate against LGBTQ+ individuals. This protection extends to all aspects of housing, including rentals, purchasing a home, advertising for housing, and access to services related to housing.

However, enforcing these laws often requires proactive steps. Documentation is key. If you believe you've experienced housing discrimination, meticulously document all interactions with landlords, real estate agents, or other parties involved in the housing transaction. This includes saving emails, text messages, letters, and any other written correspondence. Keep a detailed record of dates, times, and specific instances of discriminatory behavior. If possible, obtain witness statements from anyone who witnessed the discriminatory act. Photographs or videos can also serve as valuable evidence.

Beyond documentation, understanding your legal recourse is crucial. If you experience housing discrimination, you have several options for seeking redress. You can file a complaint with the Department of Housing and Urban Development (HUD), which is the federal agency responsible for enforcing fair housing laws. HUD investigations can lead to financial penalties for landlords or real estate agents found guilty of discrimination, and potentially monetary compensation for the victim. Additionally, many states and localities have their own fair housing agencies with parallel enforcement mechanisms. In some cases, individuals may choose to pursue legal action in civil court, where they may be able to recover damages, including monetary compensation for emotional distress, attorney's fees, and punitive damages.

Employment discrimination is another critical area where legal protections are paramount. Title VII of the Civil Rights Act of 1964, as amended, prohibits employment discrimination based on race, color, religion, sex, and national origin. While the original act didn't explicitly include sexual orientation or gender identity, numerous court cases and legislative actions at both the federal and state levels have extended this protection to LGBTQ+ individuals. The U.S. Supreme Court's landmark decision in Bostock v. Clayton County (2020) confirmed that Title VII prohibits discrimination based on sexual orientation and gender identity. This means employers cannot refuse to hire, fire, or otherwise discriminate against someone because of their sexual orientation or gender identity.

However, the legal landscape remains complex. While federal law now provides broad protection, some states still lack comprehensive anti-discrimination laws, leading to inconsistencies across the country. This necessitates careful review of state and local laws to fully understand the legal protections available in a particular jurisdiction. Furthermore, proving employment discrimination can be challenging. It often requires building a strong case that demonstrates a pattern of discriminatory behavior, showing a clear connection between the discriminatory action and the individual's sexual orientation or gender identity. Gathering evidence is crucial, including performance reviews, emails, and witness testimonies.

Legal recourse for employment discrimination includes filing a charge with the Equal Employment Opportunity Commission (EEOC), the federal agency responsible for enforcing employment discrimination laws. The EEOC will investigate the complaint and may attempt to mediate a settlement between the parties. If mediation fails, the EEOC may file a lawsuit on behalf of the individual, or the individual may choose to pursue their own legal action in court. Many states and municipalities have their own employment discrimination agencies with similar enforcement mechanisms.

Access to credit and financial services is another crucial area where LGBTQ+ individuals can face discrimination. The Equal Credit Opportunity Act (ECOA) prohibits discrimination in lending practices based on race, color, religion, national origin, sex, marital status, age, or because all or part of the applicant's income derives from a public assistance program. While ECOA does not explicitly mention sexual orientation or gender identity, many states and localities have expanded the protection to include these characteristics. This means lenders cannot deny credit, offer less favorable terms, or otherwise discriminate against LGBTQ+ individuals in their lending practices.

Discrimination in access to credit can manifest in various

ways. For instance, a lender may refuse to provide a loan, offer a higher interest rate, or impose stricter lending requirements based on an applicant's sexual orientation or gender identity. If you suspect you have experienced credit discrimination, documenting the interactions with the lender is paramount. This includes saving all correspondence, noting the dates and times of interactions, and documenting any discriminatory remarks or actions.

Legal recourse for credit discrimination includes filing a complaint with the Consumer Financial Protection Bureau (CFPB), the federal agency responsible for enforcing consumer financial protection laws, including ECOA. The CFPB will investigate the complaint and may attempt to mediate a settlement. If mediation fails, the CFPB may take enforcement action against the lender, and the individual may pursue legal action in court.

Beyond these specific legal protections, many states have enacted broader non-discrimination laws covering various aspects of public accommodation, public services, and education. These laws often prohibit discrimination based on sexual orientation and gender identity, providing additional legal safeguards for LGBTQ+ individuals. However, the specific provisions and scope of these laws vary significantly across states and jurisdictions.

Navigating the legal landscape to protect yourself from discrimination requires proactive steps, including careful documentation, understanding your legal rights, and knowing where to seek recourse. Consulting with an attorney specializing in LGBTQ+ rights can provide invaluable support and guidance in navigating the legal complexities and ensuring your rights are protected. Remember, asserting your rights is not only about seeking justice for past wrongs; it's also about building a more equitable and just society for all. The fight for equality requires ongoing vigilance and a commitment to holding institutions accountable for discriminatory practices.

Retirement Planning for The Lgbt Q Community

Retirement planning is a critical aspect of financial security, and for the LGBTQ+ community, this process often presents unique challenges. While the legal landscape is evolving to offer greater protection against discrimination, the historical and ongoing realities of bias significantly impact financial stability and, consequently, the ability to save adequately for retirement. Understanding these unique challenges and implementing tailored strategies is vital to achieving a secure and comfortable retirement.

One of the most significant factors impacting LGBTQ+ retirement planning is the potential for lower lifetime earnings. Many members of the LGBTQ+ community have faced discrimination in the workplace, resulting in fewer opportunities for career advancement, lower salaries, and even job loss. This disparity in earnings compared to their heterosexual and cisgender counterparts accumulates over time, significantly reducing their retirement savings potential. This gap isn't merely about individual choices; systemic discrimination plays a crucial role. For example, a transgender individual transitioning might face temporary job loss or reduced work hours during their transition, impacting their long-term earning capacity and retirement savings. Similarly, same-sex couples who are legally married may have faced higher tax burdens or difficulties in accessing joint financial products compared to heterosexual couples, further compounding the impact of discrimination on long- term financial security.

Furthermore, the historical lack of legal recognition for same-sex relationships has had a profound impact on retirement savings. Before the legalization of same-sex marriage, many couples faced significant obstacles in accessing joint retirement accounts, beneficiary designations, and survivor benefits. This meant that individuals in same- sex relationships often had to manage their retirement planning in isolation, lacking the combined resources and collaborative decision-making that heterosexual couples could easily utilize. This also meant that in the event of the death of one partner, the surviving partner might have faced significant financial hardship due to the lack of automatic inheritance rights or survivor benefits previously unavailable to them. Even today, some LGBTQ+ individuals may still face challenges in accessing joint financial products in states with less robust protections, highlighting the ongoing need for careful planning and legal counsel.

Another crucial aspect is the later entry into stable careers. Many LGBTQ+ individuals, particularly those who were forced to conceal their identities for professional reasons, might have delayed their career trajectory or faced challenges establishing themselves in long-term professional positions. The experience of coming out could be professionally costly, resulting in job loss, career setbacks, or a persistent fear of discrimination leading to less assertive career decisions. This delayed start can significantly impact the number of years available for retirement savings accumulation, leading to a smaller nest egg at the time of retirement.

To address these unique challenges, LGBTQ+ individuals need to implement tailored strategies to maximize their retirement savings. One key strategy is to actively engage in financial planning as early as possible. Starting retirement savings early, even with smaller contributions, can leverage the power of compound interest to accumulate significant wealth over time. It is important to note that even small, regular contributions will yield better returns over a longer period than large lump sum contributions made later in life, mitigating the effects of delayed entry into stable employment. Financial planners specializing in LGBTQ+ financial planning can assist in designing a personalized strategy that incorporates these considerations and accounts for their potential lifetime earnings.

Diversifying investment strategies is also crucial. A balanced portfolio, which includes a mix of stocks, bonds, and other assets, can help mitigate the risks associated with market fluctuations. Understanding the inherent risks and rewards associated with different investment options is crucial to make informed decisions tailored to one's risk tolerance and investment horizon. It is recommended to seek advice from a qualified financial advisor to formulate an optimal investment strategy in accordance with individual financial goals.

Additionally, it's crucial to maximize all available retirement savings vehicles. This includes taking full advantage of employer-sponsored retirement plans, such as 401(k)s and 403(b)s, and contributing to individual retirement accounts (IRAs). Understanding the rules and regulations related to these vehicles, including contribution limits and tax implications, is vital for maximizing savings.

Beyond maximizing savings, it's equally important to plan for healthcare costs in retirement. The Affordable Care Act (ACA) provides some protections against healthcare discrimination, but LGBTQ+ individuals might still face challenges accessing affordable and comprehensive healthcare coverage. Furthermore, healthcare costs often rise significantly in retirement, making careful financial planning for these expenses essential. Incorporating specific healthcare planning strategies into their broader retirement financial plan is crucial to mitigating potential financial burdens in later life. This might involve exploring options such as Medicare supplemental insurance or long-term care insurance.

Estate planning is another critical component of retirement planning for LGBTQ+ individuals. This involves creating or updating a will, establishing trusts, and designating beneficiaries for retirement accounts and other assets. This is especially important to protect same-sex partners or other chosen family members who are not automatically granted legal inheritance rights in some jurisdictions or without specific legal documentation. It's crucial to work with an attorney experienced in LGBTQ+ estate planning to ensure that your assets are distributed according to your wishes and that your chosen family members are protected. The legal complexities surrounding inheritance can be significant, and obtaining specialized legal advice can be indispensable in minimizing tax liabilities and ensuring that assets are passed on as intended.

It's also vital to be aware of the specific tax implications for LGBTQ+ couples and individuals. Tax laws can be complex, and specific circumstances may require careful tax planning to minimize tax liabilities and maximize retirement savings. A financial advisor familiar with LGBTQ+ financial needs can provide guidance to optimize tax strategies, taking into account specific situations and legal realities.

Finally, building a strong support network is invaluable. Joining LGBTQ+ financial planning groups or connecting with organizations that offer financial literacy programs can provide valuable resources, information, and emotional support. The shared experience and support from community members can create a safe and informative space for planning for the future. Such initiatives foster peer-to- peer support, providing valuable advice and reducing the sense of isolation frequently experienced while navigating complex financial matters.

In conclusion, retirement planning for the LGBTQ+ community necessitates a holistic approach that considers the unique challenges and opportunities they face. By proactively addressing potential financial disparities, maximizing available resources, and obtaining the appropriate professional advice, members of the LGBTQ+ community can build a secure financial foundation for a comfortable and fulfilling retirement. Actively engaging with financial professionals who understand and champion the needs of the LGBTQ+ community is a crucial step in achieving this goal, enabling the development of tailored strategies that account for historical and ongoing systemic discrimination while fostering financial empowerment and security for a happy retirement.

Safeguarding Your Digital Assets And Privacy

The digital realm has become an inextricable part of modern life, and for the LGBTQ+ community, this is often amplified. Online spaces provide vital connections, community building, and access to services, but this increased digital footprint also presents unique vulnerabilities. Safeguarding your digital assets and privacy is not just about protecting your financial information; it's about protecting your identity, your relationships, and your sense of security. The very platforms that foster connection and support can, if not properly secured, become avenues for exploitation and financial harm.

One of the most significant risks is online scams, which are unfortunately prevalent in the digital age. These scams can take many forms, from phishing emails designed to steal personal information, to sophisticated social engineering tactics exploiting emotional vulnerabilities. The LGBTQ+ community can be particularly vulnerable to these scams due to a number of factors. For example, the relative lack of legal protections in certain areas may lead to greater anxiety over financial matters, making individuals more susceptible to scams promising quick solutions or significant returns. The heightened reliance on online dating platforms and social media increases exposure to potential scams.

Dating app scams are a particularly insidious form of online exploitation. These scams often involve building a relationship with the victim, fostering trust, and then requesting financial assistance or access to personal financial information under various pretexts. Perpetrators frequently exploit the emotional vulnerability inherent in the search for connection and belonging, and those who are already marginalized can face heightened risk. They may be more likely to trust individuals they meet online due to limited offline social networks or prior experiences of discrimination.

To combat these threats, a multi-layered approach to digital security is crucial. The first line of defense is education. Understanding common scam tactics, such as unsolicited emails promising large financial rewards or requests for personal details from unknown individuals, is crucial in preventing them. Be highly skeptical of online interactions that request financial information, regardless of how genuine the person or organization may seem. Legitimate organizations rarely seek sensitive personal information through informal channels. Never click on links or download attachments from unknown senders, as these can contain malware that infects your computer and steals your data. Regularly check your bank and credit card statements for any unauthorized activity. Any suspicious activity should be reported immediately.

Password security is another critical element. Avoid using easily guessed passwords, such as birthdays or common words, and avoid reusing the same password across multiple accounts. Instead, create strong, unique passwords for each online account, combining uppercase and lowercase letters, numbers, and symbols. Consider using a password manager to help generate and securely store complex passwords. Many password managers also offer features such as two- factor authentication, which adds an extra layer of security by requiring a second form of verification, such as a code sent to your phone, in addition to your password.

Protecting your financial information online requires a similar level of vigilance. Be cautious about sharing personal financial details online, especially through unsecured websites or email. Only access your financial accounts through secure, official websites and apps. Look for the "https" in the website address and ensure that the website has a security certificate. Be wary of any website or email that requests sensitive information through unusual means.

Regularly reviewing your online privacy settings is also vital. This includes adjusting privacy settings on social media platforms, restricting access to personal information, and limiting the visibility of your posts and updates. Understand what information you are sharing and with whom. Social media platforms often default to sharing a surprising amount of data, and it's crucial to be proactive in managing those settings. This can significantly reduce your risk of exposure to online scams and data breaches.

Beyond individual precautions, consider the security of your devices. Install reliable antivirus and anti-malware software on all your devices and keep it updated. Regularly update the operating systems and apps on your devices to patch security vulnerabilities. This is often overlooked, yet constitutes one of the most significant vulnerabilities, as many software updates include crucial security patches that close vulnerabilities hackers may exploit.

In addition to technical measures, consider the human element. Be mindful of the information you share online, even in seemingly harmless interactions. Avoid posting personal details, such as your address, phone number, or workplace, on social media platforms or public forums. Oversharing is a common pitfall for many, often motivated by a desire for connection or validation. However, the digital footprint generated can be easily exploited by malicious actors.

Another critical step is to monitor your credit reports regularly. This will help you detect any unauthorized activity and take swift action to address potential issues. Be aware of changes in your credit report and report any anomalies immediately to the relevant credit bureaus. A credit report is a valuable record of your financial history, and its timely monitoring is a crucial component of financial security and protection. There are free resources available to assist with this process.

Building and maintaining a strong support network is critical in navigating the complexities of digital security and fraud prevention. Discuss concerns and strategies with trusted friends, family members, or community organizations. Talking about these issues openly can help reduce feelings of isolation and provide a space for sharing information and resources.

Finally, remember that you are not alone. Many organizations and resources are available to provide assistance and support in the event of online scams or cyber theft. If you believe you have been a victim of a scam, report it to the appropriate authorities, such as the Federal Trade Commission (FTC) or your local law enforcement. Seek support from community organizations that specialize in assisting victims of online crime. The act of reporting itself is crucial, not just to protect yourself but also to help prevent others from falling victim.

In conclusion, safeguarding your digital assets and privacy is a crucial aspect of overall financial security for all individuals, particularly within the LGBTQ+ community. A proactive, multi-faceted approach combining technical security measures, education, and community support is vital in protecting against online scams and cyber theft. By implementing these strategies and remaining vigilant, you can significantly reduce your risk and build a more secure financial future. The digital world offers incredible opportunities for connection and community, but vigilance is essential to ensure those opportunities are not compromised by malicious actors. The protection of your digital life is an ongoing process, requiring constant attention and adaptation to evolving threats.

3

INVESTING FOR YOUR FUTURE: BUILDING LONG -TERM WEALTH

Understanding Investment Basics and Risk Tolerance

Investing your money can feel daunting, especially when you're navigating a world that hasn't always been designed with your community in mind. However, building long-term wealth is achievable and essential for securing your financial future. This section will demystify investment basics, helping you understand your risk tolerance and make informed decisions that align with your unique goals. We'll avoid jargon and focus on practical strategies.

Before we delve into specific investment options, let's address a fundamental concept: risk tolerance. This refers to your comfort level with the potential for losing money in pursuit of higher returns. It's not about being fearless or risk-averse; it's about honestly assessing your emotional and financial capacity to handle potential losses. Several factors influence your risk tolerance:

Your time horizon: How long do you plan to invest your money before needing access to it? A longer time horizon allows you to ride out market fluctuations, making higher- risk investments potentially more suitable. If you need the money in the short term, preserving capital becomes paramount, suggesting a lower-risk approach.

Your financial situation: Consider your current financial health. Do you have an emergency fund? Are you debt-free or carrying significant debt? If you have limited savings or substantial debt, a more conservative investment strategy is generally advised. Prioritizing debt reduction and building an emergency fund should precede significant investment.

Your personality and emotional response to risk: Some individuals are naturally more comfortable with risk than others. Reflect on your past experiences with investing or financial decision-making. How did you react to losses or market volatility? Understanding your emotional response to risk is crucial for making rational investment choices. It's essential to choose a strategy that aligns with your temperament, so you can stick with it through market ups and downs.

Your financial goals: What are you investing for? Retirement? A down payment on a home? A child's education? Your goals will influence your investment timeframe and risk tolerance. Short-term goals often require a more conservative approach, while long-term goals provide more flexibility to incorporate higher-risk investments.

Once you've assessed your risk tolerance, you can begin exploring various investment options. These are broadly categorized as:

Low-risk investments: These generally offer lower returns but also pose less risk to your principal. Examples include savings accounts, money market accounts, certificates of deposit (CDs), and government bonds. These options are ideal for preserving capital and providing liquidity, particularly for short-term goals or emergency funds. While returns may not outpace inflation, they offer security and stability. The interest earned is typically modest, reflecting the lower risk.

Medium-risk investments: These involve a moderate level of risk and offer the potential for higher returns than low-risk investments. Examples include diversified mutual funds, index funds, and balanced mutual funds that blend stocks and bonds. Mutual funds pool money from multiple investors to invest in a diversified portfolio of securities, reducing individual risk. Index funds track a specific market index, like the S&P 500, providing broad market exposure. Balanced funds offer a blend of stocks and bonds, aiming for a balance between growth and stability.

High-risk investments: These carry a significantly higher risk of loss but also offer the potential for substantial returns. Examples include individual stocks, options, and real estate. Individual stocks are highly volatile and depend on the performance of a single company. Options are derivative instruments offering the right, but not the obligation, to buy or sell an asset at a specified price. Real estate investments can provide substantial returns but require significant capital outlay and involve ongoing responsibilities. High-risk investments are generally not suitable for individuals with low risk tolerance or limited financial resources. They're often considered for long-term goals where potential high rewards outweigh the risk.

Within each category, various factors influence investment performance. Diversification, the process of spreading investments across different asset classes, is critical for mitigating risk. By investing in a range of assets, you reduce the impact of any single investment underperforming. This is especially important in turbulent market conditions.

Furthermore, it's vital to consider fees associated with

investing. Many investment products charge management fees, transaction fees, or expense ratios. These fees can significantly impact your overall returns over time, so it's crucial to understand and compare these costs before investing. Consider low-cost index funds or ETFs as a way to minimize fees.

For the LGBTQ+ community, financial planning takes on added significance. Historical and ongoing discrimination has created unique challenges in wealth accumulation. This underscores the importance of proactive financial planning and seeking guidance from financial professionals who understand the specific concerns faced by our community. A trusted advisor can help you navigate the complexities of investment options, tailored to your risk tolerance, financial situation, and personal goals.

Consider the following LGBTQ+ specific considerations:

Estate planning: This is paramount, especially given legal complexities surrounding same-sex marriage and partnership recognition across jurisdictions. A well- structured estate plan protects your assets and ensures they are distributed according to your wishes. This might include wills, trusts, power of attorney documents, and healthcare directives.

Discrimination and bias: Sadly, members of the LGBTQ+ community still face discrimination in employment, housing, and access to financial services. Understanding potential biases in financial products or services is crucial to ensure you're receiving fair and equitable treatment.

Community-focused financial advisors: Seek out advisors with expertise and sensitivity towards the LGBTQ+ community. They can help navigate specific financial challenges faced by our community and provide culturally competent advice.

Long-term care planning: The costs of long-term care can be substantial, potentially depleting savings and assets. Planning for long-term care is especially important as our community often faces higher rates of chronic health conditions.

Investment decisions should be guided by your individual circumstances and goals. It’s not a one-size-fits-all approach. There is no ‘best’ investment for everyone. What works for one individual might be inappropriate for another. It is highly recommended to consult with a financial advisor to discuss your personal circumstances, risk tolerance, and financial goals before making any investment decisions. This should be an ongoing process, adapting your strategy as your needs and circumstances evolve.

Beyond the financial aspects, investing is about building a secure future for yourself, establishing financial independence, and achieving your dreams. It's about empowering yourself and your community. By understanding basic investment concepts, managing risk, and seeking support from trusted professionals, you can create a plan that fosters financial well-being and provides security for years to come. Remember, your financial success is within reach, and your unique circumstances and perspective enrich the tapestry of financial planning. Don't be afraid to seek support and advocate for your financial needs. Your journey to financial security starts with knowledge and self-advocacy. The resources and support systems are available – take advantage of them and build the future you deserve.

Diversification and Portfolio Management

Diversification is the cornerstone of sound investment strategy, and it's particularly crucial for the LGBTQ+ community, given the historical and ongoing financial inequities we face. Simply put, diversification means spreading your investments across different asset classes to reduce risk. Rather than putting all your eggs in one basket, you're distributing them among several, lessening the impact if one basket breaks. This strategy helps to cushion against market volatility and unexpected downturns.

The most common approach to diversification is asset allocation, which involves dividing your investment portfolio among different asset classes such as stocks, bonds, real estate, and cash equivalents. The ideal allocation depends entirely on your individual circumstances – your risk tolerance, time horizon, and financial goals. There's no one- size-fits-all solution. For example, a younger investor with a long time horizon before retirement might tolerate a higher allocation to stocks, seeking higher potential returns, while an older investor closer to retirement might prefer a more conservative allocation with a greater proportion in bonds and less volatile assets.

Let's delve into the main asset classes:

Stocks (Equities): Stocks represent ownership shares in a company. They are generally considered higher-risk investments but offer the potential for higher returns over the long term. Stocks can be further diversified by investing in different sectors (e.g., technology, healthcare, energy), company sizes (large-cap, mid-cap, small-cap), and geographic regions (domestic, international, emerging markets). Investing in a diversified portfolio of stocks can mitigate the risk associated with individual companies underperforming.

Bonds (Fixed Income): Bonds are loans you make to governments or corporations. They are generally considered lower-risk investments than stocks, offering a fixed income stream (interest payments) and a return of principal at maturity. Bonds offer stability and can help to balance out the volatility of stocks in a portfolio. Diversification within bonds can include investing in different maturities (short- term, intermediate-term, long-term), credit ratings (investment-grade, high-yield), and issuers (government, corporate, municipal).

Real Estate: Real estate investments can include residential properties, commercial properties, or real estate investment trusts (REITs). Real estate can provide diversification benefits and potential for long-term capital appreciation, rental income, and tax advantages. However, it's important to remember that real estate investments require significant capital outlay and often involve ongoing management responsibilities.

Cash Equivalents: Cash equivalents are highly liquid investments that offer easy access to your money. Examples include savings accounts, money market accounts, and certificates of deposit (CDs). Cash equivalents are generally low-risk investments, providing a safe haven for your funds, but they typically offer lower returns than other asset classes. A certain amount of cash is vital for emergencies and unexpected expenses. It's a crucial part of a well-rounded portfolio.

The process of constructing a portfolio involves determining the appropriate allocation of assets within your chosen asset classes based on your unique financial situation and risk tolerance. Let's examine some strategies Strategic Asset Allocation: This involves establishing a target allocation based on your long-term financial goals and risk tolerance. This allocation is regularly rebalanced to maintain the desired proportions, buying low and selling high.

Tactical Asset Allocation: This involves actively adjusting the portfolio's asset allocation in response to changes in market conditions and economic forecasts. This strategy is more active and requires more frequent monitoring and adjustments.

Core-Satellite Approach: This approach blends a core portfolio of low-cost, passively managed index funds with a satellite portfolio of actively managed funds or individual securities chosen for specific investment opportunities. This allows for diversification while balancing active and passive investment strategies.

For LGBTQ+ individuals, considering the unique challenges we face is essential when developing a diversification strategy. Access to capital, discrimination in the financial sector, and the impact of systemic inequities should all be taken into consideration.

LGBTQ+ Specific Considerations for Diversification:

Estate Planning: A well-structured estate plan is crucial for protecting your assets and ensuring they are distributed according to your wishes. This is especially vital for same-sex couples, given the complexities and variations in legal recognition across jurisdictions. Consider trusts, wills, and power of attorney designations. Your estate planning should also include provisions for long-term care, which is particularly relevant in light of higher rates of chronic illness in some segments of the LGBTQ+ community.

Access to Financial Services: Historically, access to

equitable financial services has been limited for many members of the LGBTQ+ community. This includes mortgage lending, access to credit, and investment opportunities. Actively seeking out financial institutions and advisors that demonstrate a commitment to diversity and inclusion is paramount.

Financial Literacy: Ensuring a solid understanding of financial concepts, investment strategies, and managing risk is crucial. This is particularly important given the potential for bias and discrimination in financial advice. Seek out reputable resources and educational opportunities tailored to the LGBTQ+ community's needs.

Community-Focused Advisors: Find an advisor who understands the unique financial challenges faced by the LGBTQ+ community. These professionals can provide culturally competent and sensitive advice. It's about finding a financial partner who understands not just the numbers, but your life context and concerns.

Long-Term Goals: Given potential income disparities and other inequalities, setting long-term goals and creating a diversified investment strategy to reach them is essential. This requires a plan that not only accounts for potential obstacles but also leverages opportunities for growth.

Practical Tools and Resources:

Many online resources and tools can assist in portfolio

diversification. These include:

Online portfolio trackers: Many free or subscription-based online tools allow you to track the performance of your investments across different asset classes.

Asset allocation calculators: These calculators help determine an appropriate asset allocation based on your risk tolerance, time horizon, and financial goals.

Financial planning software: Sophisticated software packages can assist with detailed financial planning, including portfolio management and retirement planning.

Financial advisors: While the tools mentioned above are helpful, the personalized guidance of a qualified financial advisor who is familiar with LGBTQ+ financial issues is invaluable.

Remember, diversification is not a one-time event; it's an ongoing process. As your circumstances, goals, and risk tolerance change over time, your portfolio should adapt accordingly. Regularly review and rebalance your portfolio to ensure it aligns with your evolving financial needs. Don't be afraid to seek expert advice, and remember that building a secure financial future is an achievable goal, especially when you have the right knowledge and support system in place. Your financial journey is unique; embrace it and navigate it with confidence.

Investing Ethically and Responsibly

Investing ethically and responsibly is increasingly important for many individuals, and for members of the LGBTQ+ community, it often holds a particularly resonant significance. It's about more than just maximizing returns; it's about aligning your investments with your values and contributing to a world that is more equitable and inclusive. This section delves into the world of socially responsible investing (SRI) and impact investing, offering pathways to build wealth while supporting causes and companies that reflect your commitment to LGBTQ+ rights and broader social justice.

Socially responsible investing (SRI) encompasses a range of strategies that consider environmental, social, and governance (ESG) factors in addition to traditional financial metrics. Instead of solely focusing on profit maximization, SRI aims to generate positive social and environmental impact alongside financial returns. This approach allows you to invest in companies that demonstrate strong ESG performance, aligning your investments with your values while mitigating risks associated with poor social or environmental practices. For example, you might choose to invest in companies with strong records on diversity and inclusion, those that actively support LGBTQ+ employee rights, or those committed to reducing their carbon footprint. Many rating agencies now provide ESG scores for publicly traded companies, enabling investors to easily identify those aligned with their values.

Impact investing takes this a step further. While SRI aims to minimize negative impact and integrate ESG factors, impact investing actively seeks to generate measurable positive social and environmental impact alongside a financial return. Impact investments are typically made in organizations dedicated to solving specific social or environmental challenges, such as affordable housing, LGBTQ+ health initiatives, or renewable energy projects. These investments can take various forms, including venture capital, private equity, and community development financial institutions (CDFIs).

Finding opportunities for impact investing that specifically benefit the LGBTQ+ community might require more research and due diligence. However, several organizations and initiatives focus on financing projects with demonstrable positive impacts on LGBTQ+ individuals and communities. For example, you might research funds specifically focused on supporting LGBTQ+-owned businesses or organizations tackling issues such as LGBTQ+ homelessness or healthcare disparities. There are also a growing number of impact bonds designed to address specific social problems, some of which may relate to improving outcomes for LGBTQ+ individuals.

Understanding the nuances of SRI and impact investing is

crucial. While the promise of financial returns coupled with social good is appealing, it's imperative to remember that impact investing can be riskier than traditional investments. Thorough research and due diligence are necessary to ensure that the investment aligns with your financial goals and the claimed social impact is credible and measurable. Don't hesitate to seek advice from a financial advisor specializing in impact investing, and insist on transparency regarding the investment's intended impact and how its progress will be tracked and reported.

Several key factors to consider when evaluating SRI and impact investing opportunities:

Transparency and Reporting: Look for investment vehicles that provide clear and transparent information on their ESG performance and social impact. Ask about the metrics used to measure success and request regular updates on the progress toward achieving the stated goals. How are they measuring their impact, and is there a credible third-party verification process?

Alignment with Your Values: Ensure that the investment

targets are consistent with your personal values and priorities. Are they actively supporting LGBTQ+ causes? Are their diversity and inclusion policies meaningful and impactful? Do their environmental practices demonstrate a genuine commitment to sustainability?

Financial Returns: While impact investing aims to generate both financial and social returns, it's still crucial to assess the financial viability of the investment. Don't put your financial security at risk solely for the sake of social impact. Balance social impact with a realistic assessment of risk and potential returns.

Due Diligence: Conduct thorough research into the organizations or companies in which you are considering investing. Check their track record, their leadership, their commitment to transparency, and their alignment with your values. Look for independent reviews and ratings to assess their credibility.

Diversification: Remember the importance of diversification, even when it comes to impact investing. Don't put all your eggs in one basket. Diversify your portfolio across different impact investments and asset classes to mitigate risk.

Beyond individual investments, consider supporting organizations that advocate for LGBTQ+ financial inclusion and economic empowerment. Many non-profits work to increase access to capital, financial literacy programs, and entrepreneurial opportunities within the LGBTQ+ community. These organizations often rely on donations and grants, and your contributions can have a significant ripple effect. Even small contributions can help create a stronger, more equitable financial landscape for LGBTQ+ individuals.

In addition to direct investment, consider the indirect ways your financial decisions can support your values. For example, you might prioritize banking with institutions that have strong LGBTQ+ inclusion policies and actively support LGBTQ+ causes. You might choose to invest your retirement savings in funds that screen out companies with poor human rights records, those involved in weapons manufacturing, or those contributing to environmental degradation.

The financial landscape is evolving to include more opportunities to invest ethically and responsibly. The growing demand for ESG investing and impact investing is driving innovation and creating more options for individuals who want to make a positive impact through their investment decisions. Don't be afraid to explore these options; they offer a powerful way to build wealth and contribute to a more just and equitable future.

Remember, integrating ethical and responsible investing into your overall financial strategy requires ongoing vigilance and evaluation. The landscape of ethical business practices and social impact investing is dynamic, so regularly review your investments to ensure they continue to align with your values and remain financially sound. By actively engaging in ethical investing, you not only contribute to positive social change but also enhance your own financial well-being by aligning your money with your values and priorities. You're not just building wealth; you're building a better future. And for members of the LGBTQ+ community, this can be especially meaningful, fostering a sense of purpose and empowerment alongside financial security. Your financial decisions are a powerful tool, allowing you to shape a world that is more just and inclusive for all.

Furthermore, actively seeking out financial advisors and institutions that prioritize diversity, equity, and inclusion is vital. Many financial institutions have made a conscious effort to improve their services and create more inclusive environments. By choosing to work with LGBTQ+-affirming professionals and institutions, you are supporting a system that works towards greater equity for everyone. This active participation in creating inclusive economic systems is a crucial component of achieving long-term financial security within a socially just and equitable framework. In addition to your personal investments, actively support organizations focused on LGBTQ+ economic empowerment. Your contributions can create a more positive and supportive financial landscape for generations to come. Your financial decisions should be a reflection of your values, and integrating responsible and ethical considerations into your investment strategy ensures that your wealth contributes to a better world. This proactive approach is essential to creating a truly inclusive and equitable future.

Long -Term Investment Strategies And Goal Setting

Long-term financial planning is crucial for building a secure and fulfilling future, especially within the context of the unique challenges and opportunities faced by the LGBTQ+ community. Setting clear, measurable, achievable, relevant, and time-bound (SMART) goals is the cornerstone of this process. These goals should reflect your personal aspirations and financial circumstances, encompassing both immediate needs and long-term ambitions.

For many, the dream of homeownership represents a significant long-term financial goal. However, navigating the complexities of the housing market can be particularly challenging for LGBTQ+ individuals, who may face discrimination or lack access to equal opportunities. Therefore, carefully planning your path to homeownership, including saving for a down payment, understanding mortgage options, and researching neighborhoods that offer a welcoming and inclusive environment, is vital. Consider exploring programs and initiatives specifically designed to support LGBTQ+ homebuyers. Several non-profit organizations and community lenders work to address the unique needs of this demographic, providing resources and assistance to overcome potential barriers.

Beyond homeownership, the desire to start a family, whether through biological means, adoption, or surrogacy, presents its own set of financial considerations. The costs associated with fertility treatments, adoption fees, surrogacy arrangements, and childcare can be substantial. Early and meticulous financial planning is essential to ensure you're adequately prepared for these expenses. This includes setting aside funds in dedicated savings accounts, exploring potential financing options, and considering the long-term implications of childcare costs on your budget. Again, seeking advice from a financial advisor specializing in LGBTQ+ financial planning can prove invaluable in navigating these complex financial landscapes.

Retirement planning is another crucial aspect of long-term financial security. Many in the LGBTQ+ community face unique challenges to retirement planning, including potential discrimination in the workplace, career interruptions due to discrimination, and lower earning potential in certain sectors. It is, therefore, essential to start planning for retirement as early as possible, even if contributions are modest initially. Take advantage of employer-sponsored retirement plans such as 401(k)s and 403(b)s, maximizing contributions to receive any employer matching contributions. Consider establishing an Individual Retirement Account (IRA), such as a Roth IRA or a traditional IRA, to supplement your retirement savings. Diversify your retirement portfolio across a range of assets, including stocks, bonds, and potentially real estate, to manage risk and optimize returns over the long term. Remember to regularly review and adjust your retirement plan to account for changes in your income, expenses, and financial goals. Consider seeking guidance from a qualified financial advisor to create a personalized retirement plan tailored to your specific circumstances and risk tolerance.

Once you've identified your long-term goals, the next step is to develop a suitable investment strategy to achieve them. This involves choosing investments that align with your risk tolerance, time horizon, and financial goals. The time horizon is a crucial factor; long-term goals, like retirement, generally allow for a greater risk tolerance, enabling you to invest in assets with higher growth potential, while short- term goals require a more conservative approach.

Diversification is essential for mitigating risk and maximizing returns across your investment portfolio. Instead of concentrating investments in a single asset class, it is recommended to spread investments across different asset classes, such as stocks, bonds, real estate, and alternative investments. This reduces the impact of any single investment underperforming. Within each asset class, diversification can be further achieved through investing in a range of different companies or securities. For example, investing in a diversified stock portfolio involving different sectors (technology, healthcare, consumer goods, etc.) and market capitalization (large-cap, mid-cap, small-cap) can help to minimize your risk. Consider investing in index funds or exchange-traded funds (ETFs) to gain diversified exposure to a large number of assets with a single investment.

Investment vehicles vary widely in their level of risk and potential return. Stocks, for instance, offer higher growth potential but carry higher risk compared to bonds. Bonds generally provide lower returns but are considered less risky. Real estate investments can offer both growth potential and rental income, but require a more substantial initial investment and ongoing management. Alternative investments, such as private equity or hedge funds, may have high growth potential but can involve significant risk and liquidity constraints.

The choice of investment strategy should be tailored to your personal risk tolerance and financial goals. A risk tolerance questionnaire can help you assess your comfort level with risk, while considering your time horizon will guide you towards selecting appropriate investment vehicles. For long- term goals, you may be comfortable taking on more risk to achieve potentially higher returns, while shorter-term goals may require a more conservative approach, prioritizing capital preservation over high growth.

Regularly rebalancing your portfolio is also important to maintain your desired asset allocation. As market conditions change, the proportion of your assets held in various asset classes might shift from your intended target allocation. Rebalancing involves selling some of your higher-performing assets and buying more of your underperforming assets to restore your desired balance. This disciplined approach helps you to manage risk and capitalize on market fluctuations.

Remember, professional advice can be invaluable in navigating the intricacies of long-term investment strategies. A financial advisor can help you develop a personalized financial plan, tailored to your specific circumstances and goals. In addition, seek out advisors with expertise and sensitivity towards the LGBTQ+ community, ensuring that your unique needs and challenges are considered throughout the planning process. They can provide guidance on tax planning, estate planning, and other crucial financial decisions that support your overall long-term financial success. Regularly reviewing your investment strategy and seeking professional advice when needed is crucial for ensuring you remain on track towards achieving your long-term financial goals.

Furthermore, consider exploring specific investment opportunities that align with your values and contribute to positive social impact within the LGBTQ+ community. Impact investing, which actively seeks to generate measurable positive social and environmental impact alongside financial returns, is a powerful tool for both financial growth and social change. Research organizations and initiatives supporting LGBTQ+-owned businesses, addressing issues such as LGBTQ+ homelessness or healthcare disparities, or promoting LGBTQ+ equality. This approach allows you to invest your money in a way that reflects your values and contributes to a more inclusive and equitable society.

Beyond formal investment strategies, building strong financial habits is equally crucial for long-term success. Develop a budget and track your expenses carefully, identifying areas where you can save and reduce unnecessary spending. Prioritize debt reduction, particularly high-interest debt, to free up more funds for investment. Learn about smart financial practices like saving and investing regularly, and consider additional forms of income generation if needed. These seemingly small steps, combined with well-planned investments, form a strong foundation for building long-term wealth. Remember that building financial security is a journey, not a destination. By remaining informed, proactive, and seeking guidance from qualified professionals, you can significantly increase your chances of achieving your financial dreams and building a more secure and fulfilling future.

Navigating The World of Financial Advisors

Finding the right financial advisor is a crucial step in securing your financial future, especially within the LGBTQ+ community where specific needs and challenges often require specialized expertise. The process of selecting an advisor shouldn't be taken lightly; it's an investment in your financial well-being and requires careful consideration. This section will guide you through the process of finding, vetting, and building a strong working relationship with a financial advisor who understands and respects your unique circumstances.

Begin by identifying your specific financial needs and goals. Are you looking for assistance with retirement planning, estate planning, investment management, or a combination of these services? Clearly defining your needs will help you narrow your search and focus on advisors with the appropriate expertise. Consider factors like your risk tolerance, investment timeline, and desired level of involvement in the investment process. This self-assessment will help you find an advisor whose approach aligns with your personality and preferences. For example, some individuals prefer a hands-on approach where they actively participate in investment decisions, while others prefer a more passive approach where the advisor manages their portfolio independently.

Once you have a clear understanding of your needs, it's time to start your search for potential advisors. Start by leveraging your network. Talk to friends, family, and colleagues who might have experience with financial advisors. Their recommendations can provide valuable insights and perspectives. Don't hesitate to ask about their experiences, both positive and negative, and whether their advisor demonstrated an understanding of LGBTQ+ issues.

Online resources can also be incredibly helpful in your search. Websites and directories dedicated to financial

advisors often allow you to filter your search based on specific criteria, including location, specialization, and certifications. However, it's essential to conduct your own thorough research beyond simply reviewing online profiles. Look for advisors who explicitly state their commitment to serving the LGBTQ+ community. Many advisors now highlight their experience and expertise in working with this demographic on their websites or in their marketing materials.

Professional organizations can also be valuable resources. The National Association of Personal Financial Advisors (NAPFA), for example, has a directory of fee-only financial advisors, who are generally considered to be more objective in their advice. You can also search for LGBTQ+-focused financial planning organizations or networks that can connect you with advisors who understand the community's unique financial needs and challenges.

When evaluating potential advisors, don't hesitate to ask about their experience working with LGBTQ+ clients. This is crucial, as many advisors may not be fully equipped to handle the specific financial complexities often faced by LGBTQ+ individuals. Directly inquiring about their knowledge and sensitivity to these issues will allow you to assess whether they possess the necessary cultural competency to understand your unique concerns. Ask specific questions about their experience in areas such as estate planning for same-sex couples, navigating the complexities of family formation (adoption, surrogacy), or addressing issues related to discrimination in the workplace and its impact on long-term financial security.

Beyond their stated experience, scrutinize their qualifications and credentials. Check if the advisor holds relevant certifications, such as a Certified Financial Planner (CFP) designation, which indicates a high level of professional competence and adherence to ethical standards. Verify their registration with regulatory bodies such as the Securities and Exchange Commission (SEC) or the Financial Industry Regulatory Authority (FINRA) to ensure they operate within legal and ethical boundaries. Inquire about their fees and how they are structured, ensuring transparency and understanding of the costs associated with their services. Avoid advisors who use high-pressure sales tactics or who seem overly focused on selling specific products rather than providing comprehensive financial planning.

Before making a decision, schedule initial consultations with several potential advisors. This is your opportunity to gauge their personality, communication style, and overall compatibility with your needs. Consider how comfortable you feel discussing your personal financial situation with them, as trust and open communication are essential for a successful working relationship. During these consultations, ask about their approach to financial planning, their investment philosophy, and their method for communicating with clients. Observe how they respond to your questions and whether they genuinely seem interested in understanding your individual circumstances and financial aspirations.

Pay close attention to the advisor's approach to diversity, equity, and inclusion. Do they proactively address the specific financial challenges facing LGBTQ+ individuals? Do they demonstrate cultural sensitivity and an awareness of the potential for discrimination within the financial industry? A good advisor will not only acknowledge these challenges but actively work to mitigate their impact on your financial well- being. Their commitment to diversity and inclusion should extend beyond mere lip service; it should be evident in their practices and how they tailor their advice to meet your individual needs. This could include their understanding of relevant legislation impacting same-sex couples or transgender individuals, their familiarity with resources and networks specifically supporting the LGBTQ+ community, or their willingness to engage in ongoing professional development to expand their knowledge in this area.

After carefully evaluating several potential advisors, select the one that best meets your needs and with whom you feel most comfortable. Once you've made your choice, clearly define your expectations and objectives for the working relationship. Outline the specific areas where you need assistance, your desired level of involvement in the decision-making process, and your preferred communication methods. Regularly schedule review meetings to discuss your progress, address any concerns, and adjust your plan as needed. Remember that financial planning is a dynamic process; your goals and circumstances may evolve over time, requiring periodic adjustments to your strategy.

Building a strong, productive working relationship with your financial advisor is crucial for achieving your long-term financial goals. Open communication, trust, and mutual respect are essential for ensuring your financial advisor understands and addresses your unique needs. Don’t hesitate to ask questions, express your concerns, and provide feedback throughout the process. Remember, your financial advisor is a partner in your journey toward financial security, and a strong relationship will significantly increase the likelihood of achieving your aspirations. Choosing a financial advisor who understands the specific needs of the LGBTQ+ community is not just a wise financial decision; it’s an investment in your well-being and future. By carefully navigating the process outlined above, you can confidently embark on building a secure and fulfilling future.

4

MANAGING RELATIONSHIP FINANCES: SHARING RESPONSIBILITIES

Financial Transparency and Communication in Relationship

Open communication is the bedrock of any successful relationship, and this is especially true when it comes to finances. For LGBTQ+ couples, who may face unique legal and societal challenges, transparent financial discussions are not just advisable—they're essential. Ignoring financial disparities or avoiding tough conversations can lead to resentment, conflict, and ultimately, the breakdown of the relationship. This section will explore strategies for fostering open dialogue about money, establishing shared financial goals, and navigating potential disagreements.

The first step towards financial transparency is acknowledging that money is often a sensitive topic. Many individuals, regardless of their sexual orientation or gender identity, have complex relationships with money, shaped by personal experiences, family dynamics, and societal expectations. Some may have grown up in households where finances were never discussed openly, leading to a reluctance to share their own financial information with a partner. Others may harbor feelings of shame or guilt about their financial situation, making it difficult to be vulnerable with someone else.

For LGBTQ+ individuals, additional layers of complexity can arise. Financial discrimination, particularly in the workplace, can lead to financial instability and anxiety. The lack of legal recognition for same-sex marriage or partnerships in certain regions historically created hurdles in accessing joint financial products and protections. Even with increased legal protections, the fear of discrimination, particularly in accessing credit or insurance, can impact financial openness and create an environment where avoiding difficult conversations about money feels safer.

Addressing these underlying emotional issues is crucial before diving into practical strategies for financial transparency. Creating a safe and non-judgmental space for open communication is paramount. This might involve scheduling dedicated time to talk about finances, choosing a neutral and comfortable setting, and actively listening to each other's perspectives without interruption. Consider starting with smaller, less emotionally charged topics before tackling more sensitive issues. For instance, begin by discussing monthly expenses and income, gradually working towards more complex matters like debt, investments, and long-term financial goals.

One effective strategy is to create a shared budget. This doesn't necessarily mean combining all accounts; it involves collaboratively tracking income and expenses, identifying areas where spending can be adjusted, and setting realistic financial goals. Numerous budgeting apps and software programs are available to streamline this process, providing tools for tracking spending, setting budgets, and monitoring progress towards financial goals. These tools can make the process less daunting and more collaborative, transforming what might feel like a chore into a shared project.

When creating a shared budget, it's crucial to consider each individual's financial contribution, whether it's a salary, freelance income, or other sources. Equitable distribution of financial responsibilities is vital to maintaining fairness and avoiding resentment. This isn’t necessarily a 50/50 split; rather, it’s a balance that reflects the individuals’ contributions and priorities. For example, one partner might manage investments while the other handles everyday bills; one partner might earn a higher income, but both agree to contribute a certain percentage towards shared expenses.

Defining shared financial goals is equally important. Are you saving for a down payment on a house, planning for retirement, or hoping to travel the world? Clearly articulating your shared aspirations fosters a sense of unity and provides a common purpose for your joint financial efforts. These goals should be revisited and updated regularly to reflect changing circumstances and priorities. For example, adopting a child or dealing with unexpected health expenses can dramatically impact short-term and long-term financial planning.

Setting financial goals that align with your values is also crucial. This includes considering your commitment to charitable giving, sustainable living, or other causes you believe in. Integrating these values into your financial planning can make the process more meaningful and help strengthen your commitment to your shared financial vision.

Disagreements about money are inevitable in any relationship. The key is to develop healthy mechanisms for resolving these conflicts constructively. This might involve actively listening to each other's perspectives, seeking compromises, and focusing on finding solutions rather than assigning blame. Couples therapy can be invaluable in learning effective communication and conflict-resolution strategies. It provides a neutral space where a professional can help couples navigate sensitive financial conversations and develop healthier patterns of communication.

Consider exploring pre-nuptial or cohabitation agreements, especially for same-sex couples, regardless of whether there is a significant disparity in income or assets. These legal documents, far from being a sign of mistrust, can provide clarity and security, particularly if one partner has substantially more assets or has significant debts. They offer a structured framework for outlining financial expectations, ownership of assets, and distribution of property in the event of separation or death. The process of creating these agreements can also facilitate open and honest conversations about finances, which strengthens communication in the long term.

For LGBTQ+ couples, estate planning is especially critical. Intestate succession laws (the laws that govern the distribution of assets when someone dies without a will) can vary significantly across jurisdictions and may not always reflect the wishes of same-sex couples. Creating a will, power of attorney, and healthcare directive ensures that your assets are distributed according to your wishes and that your partner is legally recognized as your designated beneficiary. This process also allows you to plan for long-term care, ensuring your partner is protected in case of illness or incapacitation.

Navigating these legal aspects requires specialized expertise, and consulting with an LGBTQ+ friendly estate planning attorney is highly recommended.

Financial transparency and open communication are not merely practical steps in managing a relationship; they're foundational elements for building trust, intimacy, and long- term stability. By proactively addressing financial issues, establishing shared goals, and developing healthy conflict- resolution strategies, LGBTQ+ couples can foster strong, enduring relationships built on mutual understanding and respect. Remember that seeking professional guidance, whether from a therapist or a financial advisor, is a sign of strength, not weakness. It's an investment in the health and happiness of your relationship. Embracing financial transparency is an investment in the future of your relationship, offering greater security and allowing you to focus on shared dreams and aspirations. Open communication, a willingness to negotiate, and a recognition of the emotional undercurrents affecting financial decision- making are keys to success. The journey towards financial harmony is not always easy, but the rewards of shared financial security and transparent communication far outweigh the challenges.

Joint Accounts and Financial Decision Making

Joint accounts offer a practical way to manage shared

finances, but choosing the right type and understanding the implications are crucial. There's no one-size-fits-all solution; the best approach depends on individual circumstances, risk tolerance, and the level of financial integration desired. Let's explore the common types of joint accounts and their nuances.

Joint Tenancy with Right of Survivorship (JTWROS): This is the most common type of joint account. Upon the death of one account holder, the surviving owner automatically inherits the entire account balance. This simplifies estate administration and avoids probate, which can be a lengthy and costly legal process. However, it's crucial to understand that this arrangement offers no control over who receives the funds. Creditors of the deceased can also access the funds in the account. For LGBTQ+ couples, this can be particularly important, as it offers legal recognition of the relationship and ensures the surviving partner's financial security in the event of the death of the other partner. However, careful consideration of the potential impact on estate planning for larger assets is necessary.

Tenancy in Common (TIC): This type of account allows each owner to specify a percentage of ownership and how their share will be distributed upon their death. Unlike JTWROS, a TIC account requires the inclusion of a will designating how the deceased's share of the account will be transferred. This provides greater control over asset distribution and allows for a more tailored approach to estate planning. For instance, one partner might leave their share to a child from a previous relationship, while the other partner retains their ownership. This option offers flexibility but can be more complicated to manage. In the context of LGBTQ+ financial planning, this option allows for greater control over asset allocation and ensures that individual wishes concerning inheritance are respected.

Community Property: In community property states (primarily in the western United States), assets acquired during the marriage are equally owned by both spouses. This means that all income earned during the marriage, as well as any assets purchased with that income, are considered community property, regardless of whose name is on the account or asset. This differs from other states which follow common law property systems. In community property states, the management of a joint account often mirrors the automatic inheritance of the JTWROS account, though the underlying legal framework is different. For LGBTQ+ couples, understanding the nuances of community property laws is essential, especially if they move to or from a community property state or plan for future relocation. It is important to note that while this simplifies joint ownership in some ways, it requires a thorough understanding of the legal implications in estate planning, ensuring the rights of both parties are protected.

Financial Decision-Making within the Relationship: Once

the appropriate type of joint account is selected, it's essential to establish clear and consistent communication regarding financial decision-making. This includes deciding on the level of shared financial control. Will all major decisions be made collaboratively, or will one partner take the lead on specific financial areas, such as budgeting or investments? Defining roles and responsibilities can prevent misunderstandings and conflicts down the line. It's important to align these decisions with the couple's overall communication style and decision- making preferences. For example, a couple that values equality might opt for a 50/50 split in decision-making power, while another might prefer a more delegated approach based on individual strengths or time commitments.

For LGBTQ+ couples, this discussion is particularly critical given the historical lack of legal recognition and protection for their relationships. Establishing clear decision-making protocols ensures both partners have a voice and prevents potential power imbalances that could arise from unequal financial contributions or understanding. Regular review of financial agreements, particularly in the context of evolving relationship dynamics, is vital to maintain equity and prevent any resentment.

Navigating Disparities in Income and Assets: Significant disparities in income or assets between partners can create additional challenges. Open and honest communication about these differences is paramount, even if it feels uncomfortable. One approach might be to maintain separate accounts for personal spending, while a joint account is used for shared expenses, such as rent, utilities, and groceries. The proportion contributed to the joint account could be based on the income ratio or agreed-upon percentages. Another approach involves the higher-earning partner contributing a proportionally larger amount to savings or investment goals.

Regardless of the chosen strategy, it's crucial to regularly review and adjust the arrangement to reflect any changes in income, expenses, or individual goals. Transparency is key; both partners need to be aware of their respective financial contributions and the overall financial health of the household. Maintaining this transparency prevents misunderstandings and helps build trust and financial security.

Legal and Tax Implications: Understanding the tax implications of joint accounts is essential, particularly regarding filing status and liability for tax debts. Generally, married couples have the option to file jointly, potentially lowering their overall tax burden. However, in the event of a joint tax liability, both partners are equally responsible for the taxes owed, regardless of individual contributions to the debt. This is a crucial consideration, especially if one partner has a substantially higher income or significantly greater assets. A clear understanding of the shared financial responsibilities, including tax liabilities, needs to be established early in the relationship. Consultations with a tax professional specializing in LGBTQ+ financial planning can help navigate the complexities of tax laws and ensure compliance.

Protecting Individual Financial Autonomy: While joint accounts offer many benefits, it's important to remember the importance of maintaining a degree of individual financial autonomy. Having a separate account for personal spending allows for individual financial independence, which can be crucial for fostering self-reliance and reducing potential conflict arising from spending habits. This approach does not negate the necessity of financial transparency but rather seeks to strike a balance between shared responsibility and individual freedom. This is particularly important for LGBTQ+ individuals who might have experienced financial insecurity or control issues in the past. A healthy financial relationship recognizes the importance of individual financial space and freedom within the framework of a shared financial future.

In conclusion, carefully choosing a joint account type and establishing clear communication about financial decision- making, coupled with an awareness of legal and tax implications, are crucial steps for LGBTQ+ couples in navigating shared finances effectively. Regular review and adaptation of these arrangements ensures that the financial structure aligns with evolving needs and aspirations. Remember to consult with professionals specializing in

LGBTQ+ financial planning to receive personalized guidance tailored to your unique circumstances. They will help you navigate legal complexities, optimize your tax strategy and ensure your financial security as a couple. The path towards shared financial security and happiness is not without its hurdles, but by proactively engaging with these issues, LGBTQ+ couples can build a strong and enduring foundation for their financial future.

Pre-Nuptial Agreements and Legal Protections

Prenuptial agreements, often perceived as unromantic or indicative of a lack of trust, are in fact powerful tools for safeguarding individual financial interests and promoting clarity within a relationship. For LGBTQ+ couples, the importance of a prenuptial agreement (often referred to as a pre-nup) is magnified due to the historical lack of legal recognition for same-sex relationships and the potential complexities arising from blended families or significantly differing financial backgrounds. A well-drafted pre-nup can ensure that each partner's assets and financial contributions are clearly defined and protected, regardless of future relationship changes. It acts as a proactive measure to prevent potential disputes or misunderstandings, particularly in the event of separation or death.

The misconception that pre-nups are only necessary for couples with substantial wealth is inaccurate. Even couples with modest assets can benefit from a pre-nup. It's a matter of establishing clear expectations and protecting the financial well-being of each individual. For example, a couple where one partner owns a small business might want to protect that asset from potential claims in case of a separation. Similarly, a couple where one partner has significant student loan debt might want to protect their individual assets from the burden of that debt. The pre-nup can clearly outline how these assets and liabilities will be handled in various scenarios.

For same-sex couples, pre-nuptial agreements are especially crucial because state laws regarding property division vary significantly. In some states, common-law marriage might be recognized, even without a formal ceremony, while others may not offer the same protections for unmarried partners. A pre-nup ensures that each partner's rights are clearly defined, regardless of the legal nuances of the state they reside in. This avoids potential legal battles and ensures a fair and equitable division of assets should the relationship end.

Beyond asset protection, pre-nuptial agreements can address other critical aspects of a relationship, including:

Separate Property: A pre-nup clearly designates what assets each partner brought into the marriage and maintains as their separate property. This includes real estate, savings accounts, investments, businesses, and inheritances. Clearly defining separate property minimizes disputes concerning assets accumulated before the marriage. For couples with significant pre-marital assets, this is essential. This is especially important for LGBTQ+ individuals who may have accumulated assets independently before the legalization of same-sex marriage, ensuring those assets are protected.

Spousal Support (Alimony): The pre-nup can dictate the terms of spousal support, including its duration and amount, in the event of separation or divorce. This helps avoid costly and emotionally draining litigation later on. In cases where there's a significant income disparity, a pre-nup can ensure a fair and equitable outcome for both partners, regardless of their respective contributions to the household. The agreement can stipulate how spousal support will be handled, considering factors such as length of marriage, individual income, and needs of both partners.

Debt Allocation: Pre-nuptial agreements can address the allocation of existing debts, such as student loans or credit card debt. It clarifies which partner is responsible for which debts, protecting one partner from inheriting the other's financial obligations. This is particularly important in blended families where one partner might have existing debts from previous relationships. Clear delineation of debt responsibility prevents unexpected financial burdens for either partner in the event of separation or divorce.

Estate Planning: A pre-nup can incorporate estate planning

provisions, specifying how assets will be distributed upon the death of one partner. This ensures that the wishes of each partner are respected and avoids potential conflicts among family members. It's particularly crucial for LGBTQ+ couples, as inheritance laws can be complex and may not automatically recognize the surviving partner as the primary beneficiary. A well-structured pre-nup avoids potential family disputes or legal challenges to inheritance.

The creation of a prenuptial agreement requires careful consideration and legal expertise. It's advisable to seek legal counsel from a lawyer specializing in family law and, ideally, one with experience in LGBTQ+ financial planning. A lawyer can help you navigate the legal complexities, ensure the agreement is legally sound, and protect your rights and interests. The drafting process should involve open communication and transparency between both partners, creating a mutually agreeable and fair document.

Postnuptial agreements serve a similar purpose but are entered into after the marriage. They can be used to address changes in financial circumstances, such as inheritance, significant business ventures, or changes in career trajectory, that were not anticipated at the time of the marriage. They can also be used to create a legally binding agreement to address aspects of the marriage that were not previously addressed in a prenuptial agreement. The same legal principles and considerations apply to postnuptial agreements as to prenups, including the need for clear language, legal counsel, and open communication between partners.

For LGBTQ+ couples with blended families, pre-nuptial and postnuptial agreements take on added importance. They can address complex scenarios involving children from previous relationships, safeguarding the interests of both partners and children. The agreements can outline how assets will be distributed, ensuring fair treatment of everyone involved. It's imperative to involve all relevant parties and seek legal counsel specializing in this complex area of law.

It’s crucial to remember that a prenuptial or postnuptial agreement is not a sign of distrust but rather a proactive measure designed to protect each partner’s financial security and ensure a clear understanding of the financial implications of the relationship. It fosters open communication and provides a framework for a financially stable and equitable partnership. By proactively addressing potential financial issues, LGBTQ+ couples can focus on building a strong and lasting relationship, free from the stress and uncertainty that unresolved financial disputes can create. Professional advice is crucial in this process to navigate the potential legal complexities and ensure the agreement protects both partners fairly and effectively. Regular review of these agreements is highly recommended, as circumstances can change over time, and adjustments might be necessary to reflect these changing circumstances. Finally, remember that while legal protection is important, open and honest communication remains the cornerstone of any successful and financially sound relationship.

Managing Finances Within Chosen Families

The concept of "family" extends far beyond traditional blood ties, particularly within the LGBTQ+ community. Chosen families, built on love, loyalty, and shared experiences, often function as the primary support system for many individuals. These families, however, face unique financial challenges that require careful consideration and collaborative strategies. Unlike legally recognized familial relationships, chosen families lack the automatic legal protections and financial frameworks provided by marriage or blood relation. This necessitates proactive financial planning and open communication to ensure financial stability and mutual support.

One of the most significant challenges for chosen families is the lack of legal recognition in many financial contexts.

Inheritance laws, for example, often prioritize biological relatives, potentially leaving chosen family members with little to no legal recourse in the event of a member's death. This underscores the vital need for comprehensive estate planning, including wills, trusts, and beneficiary designations, to explicitly include chosen family members and ensure their financial security. A well-structured will can designate specific assets or portions of an estate to chosen family members, effectively circumventing potential legal roadblocks and reflecting the true wishes of the deceased. Similarly, trusts can provide a mechanism for managing assets and ensuring their distribution according to the wishes of the grantor, even after their death. Beneficiary designations on retirement accounts, life insurance policies, and other assets are equally critical, ensuring that these funds are channeled to the intended chosen family members.

Beyond estate planning, chosen families require strategies for shared financial responsibilities and resource management. This often involves open discussions about financial contributions, shared expenses, and debt management. Shared housing arrangements, for instance, require clear agreements regarding rent, utilities, and household maintenance. A written agreement outlining each member's responsibilities and financial contributions can prevent misunderstandings and maintain a harmonious living arrangement. This agreement should be comprehensive, covering all aspects of shared living, from the division of chores and responsibilities to the procedure for resolving disputes. Consider involving a neutral party, like a financial advisor or mediator, to facilitate the creation of a fair and equitable agreement, ensuring that all parties understand their obligations and rights.

Healthcare is another critical area requiring proactive planning. Chosen families often rely on one another for emotional, physical, and financial support during times of illness or medical emergencies. Health insurance coverage, access to healthcare providers, and the management of medical bills often require coordination and shared responsibility. Openly discussing health insurance options, planning for long-term care, and establishing a system for sharing medical costs can significantly ease the burden during challenging times. Exploring options like shared health insurance plans, if feasible, can offer cost savings and provide greater security. Moreover, it's prudent to establish a clear protocol for managing healthcare decisions in the event of incapacity or emergency, ensuring that the wishes of each individual are respected and their well-being is prioritized.

Financial support within chosen families can also extend to educational expenses, career transitions, and other significant life events. Establishing a system for collective savings or providing financial assistance during periods of hardship can strengthen the bonds of the chosen family and provide critical support during challenging times. This might involve the creation of a shared savings account, managed collaboratively, or the establishment of a mutual support fund for unforeseen circumstances. A transparent and well- defined system, with agreed-upon contribution levels and usage guidelines, can ensure the equitable distribution of resources and prevent disputes.

The complexities of managing finances within a chosen family are not always straightforward, particularly given the absence of legal frameworks that govern traditional family structures. The absence of legal precedence, however, necessitates a heightened level of open communication, transparency, and proactive planning. Regular family meetings dedicated to discussing financial matters, budgeting, and long-term goals can foster a sense of shared responsibility and prevent misunderstandings. These meetings should serve as a forum for openly discussing financial concerns, addressing any disagreements constructively, and ensuring that all members are informed and involved in the financial decision-making process.

While open communication is paramount, it's advisable to supplement these discussions with written agreements and formal financial planning. Consulting with a financial advisor experienced in working with chosen families can provide invaluable guidance on estate planning, investment strategies, and risk management. A financial advisor can also assist in developing a comprehensive financial plan that aligns with the shared goals and needs of the chosen family members. This plan should incorporate elements such as budgeting, savings, investment, debt management, and estate planning, tailored to the specific circumstances of the family.

Furthermore, understanding the legal landscape pertaining to chosen families is crucial. This involves researching state and local laws regarding healthcare directives, inheritance, and power of attorney. Understanding these legal parameters can help chosen families create legally sound agreements that protect their rights and ensure their financial security. Consultations with legal professionals specializing in LGBTQ+ legal issues can provide vital insights and guidance in this area.

It is essential to remember that building a financially secure chosen family is an ongoing process that requires continuous communication, adaptation, and a willingness to work collaboratively. The absence of traditional legal structures necessitates greater proactive planning and a heightened awareness of the legal and financial implications of shared responsibilities. By embracing open communication, formalizing agreements, and seeking professional guidance, chosen families can navigate the unique financial challenges they face and build a strong foundation for lasting financial stability and mutual support. This is crucial for safeguarding their collective well-being and ensuring the longevity of their chosen family bonds. Remember that building financial security within a chosen family is not simply about managing money; it's about fostering a deeper sense of trust, commitment, and shared responsibility, all of which contribute to the overall health and well-being of the family unit. Proactive financial planning, coupled with open communication and professional guidance, is the key to building a strong and financially secure chosen family. It’s a testament to the power of love, commitment, and the resilience of the chosen family structure.

The importance of periodic reviews of these agreements and financial plans cannot be overstated. Life circumstances change – individuals may experience career shifts, inheritances, or significant life events – impacting their financial landscape. These changes necessitate regular assessments of the chosen family's financial situation and adjustments to the existing agreements and plans. This periodic review ensures that the chosen family's financial strategies remain aligned with their evolving needs and circumstances. Regular consultations with a financial advisor or legal professional can ensure that these adjustments are made correctly and that the family remains legally and financially protected. Such consistent diligence ensures not only the long-term financial security of the chosen family, but also contributes to the continued strength and stability of the bonds that unite them. It underscores a commitment to mutual support and demonstrates the enduring nature of the chosen family.

Navigating Financial Disagreements

Navigating the complexities of shared finances within any relationship requires a delicate balance of trust, transparency, and open communication. However, for LGBTQ+ couples and families, these challenges can be amplified by societal biases, unique legal considerations, and the often-uncharted territory of navigating finances within non-traditional family structures. Disagreements are inevitable, and the key lies not in avoiding conflict, but in developing healthy strategies for resolving them constructively.

One common source of friction revolves around differing financial philosophies. Perhaps one partner is a meticulous saver, prioritizing long-term security, while the other prefers a more spontaneous approach, valuing immediate gratification. These differing perspectives aren't inherently problematic; the issue arises when these differences aren't acknowledged and addressed openly. Openly discussing individual financial goals, risk tolerance, and spending habits is the foundation for a healthy financial partnership. This isn't a one-time conversation but an ongoing dialogue requiring regular check-ins and adjustments as life circumstances evolve. Consider creating a shared budget together, using budgeting apps or spreadsheets to track income, expenses, and savings goals. Visualizing your shared finances can make the discussion more concrete and help identify areas of potential conflict.

Another frequent source of disagreement centers around debt management. Pre-existing debt from before the relationship, or debt incurred jointly during the relationship, can create tension if not handled collaboratively. Transparency is key: both partners need a clear understanding of the total debt, the interest rates, and repayment plans. Developing a unified strategy for debt repayment, prioritizing high-interest debts, and exploring options like debt consolidation, can alleviate stress and foster a sense of shared responsibility. Involving a financial advisor specializing in debt management can provide objective guidance and help develop a tailored repayment plan that aligns with your shared financial goals. Remember to approach this conversation with empathy and understanding; focusing on collaborative solutions rather than blame will foster a more productive discussion.

Similarly, significant purchases, whether a new car, a house, or a significant investment, often require careful consideration and compromise. Before making such purchases, engage in thorough discussions about affordability, long-term implications, and the alignment with your shared financial goals. Establishing clear guidelines for major purchases, perhaps setting a spending threshold that requires mutual agreement, can prevent impulsive decisions and potential disagreements. This collaborative approach will not only enhance financial stability but also strengthen your bond through shared decision-making. Financial planning software or apps can help model the impact of such purchases, providing a clear picture of their effect on your financial health.

Disagreements around inheritance or estate planning can also be particularly sensitive within LGBTQ+ relationships, where legal recognition may be less straightforward than in heterosexual marriages. Openly discussing inheritance plans, ensuring both partners feel secure and valued in the long- term, is crucial. This may involve updating wills, creating trusts, or designating beneficiaries on various accounts to reflect your relationship and shared intentions. Consulting with an estate planning attorney specializing in LGBTQ+ legal matters is crucial to ensure that your wishes are legally protected and that your partner's rights are secured. This proactive approach minimizes future misunderstandings and ensures your partner is protected regardless of legal complexities.

Beyond financial specifics, the emotional aspects of money conflicts shouldn't be ignored. Often, financial disagreements stem from deeper issues like feelings of control, insecurity, or power imbalances. Addressing the underlying emotional factors can be just as important as tackling the financial details. Consider couples therapy or financial counseling to help you navigate these deeper issues and develop healthier communication patterns. A skilled therapist or counselor can provide a safe space to unpack your feelings, work through misunderstandings, and develop strategies for communicating more effectively. Addressing emotional factors proactively can prevent minor financial disagreements from escalating into larger relationship conflicts.

When disagreements persist despite attempts at resolution, seeking professional help is crucial. A financial advisor can provide objective guidance on budgeting, debt management, investment strategies, and long-term financial planning. Their expertise can help you develop a financial plan that aligns with your shared goals and values, offering a neutral perspective on potentially contentious issues. Mediation, a structured process involving a neutral third party, can also be beneficial in resolving complex financial disputes. A mediator helps facilitate communication, guiding you toward a mutually agreeable solution. This approach can be particularly helpful when emotions are running high and direct communication is challenging.

Finally, remember that financial planning is an ongoing process, not a one-time event. Regularly reviewing your budget, financial goals, and investment strategies ensures that your plan remains aligned with your evolving needs and circumstances. Schedule regular financial check-ins, similar to scheduled medical appointments, to ensure that you are proactively managing your finances and addressing any potential issues before they escalate. This approach not only strengthens your financial stability but also reinforces the commitment and partnership at the heart of your relationship. Open communication, combined with professional guidance when needed, is crucial for building a secure and harmonious financial life together. Don't underestimate the power of proactive planning and open dialogue; they are the cornerstones of financial stability and a lasting, supportive relationship. Seeking help is a sign of strength, not weakness; it demonstrates a commitment to resolving conflicts constructively and preserving the financial well-being of your relationship. Remember that financial harmony is intricately linked to the overall health and well- being of your relationship, and proactive planning ensures the long-term success of both.

5

HOME OWNERSHIP AND REAL ESTATE: BUILDING EQUITY

Understanding The Home Buying Process

The journey to homeownership, a significant milestone for many, presents a unique set of challenges and opportunities within the LGBTQ+ community. While the process itself remains largely the same, navigating the complexities of mortgages, down payments, and closing costs often requires a more nuanced approach, particularly given the potential for discriminatory practices and the specific financial realities faced by many LGBTQ+ individuals and couples. This section will provide a practical, step-by-step guide to buying a home, addressing common concerns and offering strategies for mitigating potential risks.

First and foremost, securing pre-approval for a mortgage is paramount. This crucial step involves providing lenders with your financial information, including credit score, income, debts, and assets. Pre-approval not only informs you of how much you can realistically borrow but also strengthens your negotiating position when making offers on homes. Crucially, be aware that lenders may inadvertently or intentionally discriminate based on your sexual orientation or gender identity. While protected under federal fair lending laws, subtle biases can still emerge, leading to less favorable terms or outright rejection. Choosing a lender with a strong reputation for inclusivity and fair lending practices is therefore essential. Consider seeking referrals from LGBTQ+ organizations or financial advisors experienced in working with this demographic. Don't hesitate to ask prospective lenders directly about their policies and commitment to equitable lending practices. A thorough understanding of your credit score and report is equally important. A low credit score can significantly limit your borrowing options and result in higher interest rates. It's essential to review your credit report regularly and address any inaccuracies or negative marks. If you have experienced discrimination in the past that has affected your credit, documentation of this can be invaluable when addressing potential biases with lenders.

Next, determining your budget and saving for a down

payment is crucial. The required down payment varies depending on the type of mortgage and lender, but a larger down payment usually translates to lower monthly payments and a more favorable interest rate. While the traditional 20% down payment is often cited, various loan programs exist that require less, including FHA and VA loans, which may be particularly beneficial to first-time homebuyers or those with less capital. Research these options thoroughly to find the best fit for your circumstances. However, remember that even with a smaller down payment, you may face higher interest rates or additional fees, so budgeting diligently is vital. Creating a realistic budget that accounts for not only the down payment but also closing costs, property taxes, home insurance, and potential maintenance expenses is essential. Overlooking these recurring expenses can severely impact your financial stability post-purchase. Consider consulting with a financial advisor experienced in homeownership to develop a comprehensive budget tailored to your needs and financial capabilities. For same-sex couples, ensuring both partners are included in the financial planning is especially important, given the potential legal complexities that may arise in the case of unexpected circumstances.

The process of finding a suitable home often involves considerable time and effort. Working with a real estate agent familiar with your community and your needs can significantly streamline the search. An LGBTQ+-inclusive real estate agent will understand the specific needs and priorities of the community, including an understanding of neighborhood safety and acceptance. Furthermore, working with a real estate agent provides an additional layer of protection against potential housing discrimination. They can help to navigate the complexities of the housing market and ensure that the process is as transparent and fair as possible. During the search, be cautious of any potential biases or discriminatory practices. If you feel uncomfortable or experience discriminatory behavior from a seller or landlord, document everything and report it to the appropriate authorities. It's advisable to keep detailed records of all communication and interactions. This documentation can be immensely valuable if you need to pursue legal remedies.

Once you've found a suitable home and made an offer, the process of negotiating terms begins. This phase often involves careful consideration of various factors, including the purchase price, contingencies, and closing costs. Having a pre-approved mortgage significantly strengthens your negotiating position. A real estate attorney specialized in real estate transactions is recommended to review all documents and ensure that your rights are protected throughout the process. An attorney can also help you navigate any complexities specific to your legal status, such as being in a same-sex marriage or partnership, which may have implications for property ownership and tax implications. Remember that many additional costs beyond the purchase price are associated with buying a home, including closing costs, which can range from 2% to 5% of the purchase price. These costs include appraisal fees, title insurance, loan origination fees, and other various administrative charges. Planning for these expenses is essential to avoid unforeseen financial strain.

The final stages of home buying involve the appraisal, inspection, and closing processes. The appraisal determines the fair market value of the property, ensuring that the agreed-upon price aligns with the property's actual worth. A home inspection identifies any potential structural or mechanical problems, allowing you to negotiate repairs with the seller or adjust the purchase price accordingly. The closing process involves the finalization of the transaction, where all relevant documents are signed, and funds are exchanged. Once again, legal counsel is invaluable at this stage, ensuring that all documents are reviewed thoroughly and that you are protected from any potential legal issues. Navigating the closing process can seem daunting, but having a skilled legal and financial team provides the necessary support and expertise to ensure a smooth and successful transition to homeownership.

Beyond the practical steps, emotional factors significantly influence the home-buying journey. The process can be stressful, particularly when dealing with potential discrimination or financial challenges. Maintaining open communication with your partner, family, or friends can help to manage stress levels and provide much-needed support. Regular check-ins and honest conversations are crucial to navigating the emotional ups and downs that accompany such a significant life event. Remember that seeking professional help is a sign of strength, not weakness, and accessing resources such as financial advisors or therapists can provide essential emotional and practical support.

Finally, homeownership is not simply a financial transaction but also a significant personal investment, representing a substantial step in building financial security and long-term stability. For LGBTQ+ individuals and couples, this can be particularly meaningful, given the historical and ongoing challenges faced in achieving financial security and building a family. Understanding the complexities of the process, preparing diligently, and seeking expert guidance when needed empowers you to navigate the path to homeownership successfully and achieve this important milestone with confidence and pride. Remember to prioritize your well-being throughout the entire process.

Finding an LGBTQ Friendly Real Estate Agent

Finding the right real estate agent is crucial for a smooth and positive home-buying experience. This is especially true for LGBTQ+ individuals and couples who may face unique challenges and require an agent who understands and addresses those concerns. While the process of buying a home remains largely the same, the complexities are amplified when navigating potential discrimination and ensuring a fair and inclusive experience. Therefore, selecting a real estate agent who is not only competent but also actively committed to supporting the LGBTQ+ community is paramount.

One of the most effective ways to find an LGBTQ+-friendly real estate agent is through referrals and networking within your community. Connect with LGBTQ+ organizations, community centers, and social groups in your area. These organizations often maintain lists of professionals who are known for their inclusivity and sensitivity. Talking to friends, family, colleagues, or members of your community who have recently purchased homes can provide valuable firsthand accounts and recommendations. Word-of-mouth referrals can be incredibly powerful and often lead to agents who have a proven track record of successfully representing LGBTQ+ clients. Don’t hesitate to ask specific questions about their experiences working with LGBTQ+ clients, and if possible, ask for contact information of previous clients for testimonials.

Online resources can also prove beneficial in your search. Many real estate websites now allow you to filter agents based on their specialties and affiliations. While there isn't a universally recognized "LGBTQ+-friendly" designation, you can look for agents who explicitly mention their commitment to diversity and inclusion in their profiles or marketing materials. Additionally, searching online for "LGBTQ+- inclusive real estate agents" within your specific geographic area might yield relevant results. Pay close attention to the agent's website and social media presence. A commitment to diversity and inclusion is often reflected in the imagery, language, and overall tone of their online materials. Look for agents whose websites and social media profiles showcase diversity and actively promote their commitment to fair housing practices.

However, relying solely on online profiles can be limiting. Therefore, it is vital to conduct thorough due diligence before engaging an agent. Schedule introductory calls or meetings with several potential candidates to assess their understanding of the unique challenges faced by LGBTQ+ clients. During these conversations, ask direct questions to gauge their level of awareness and commitment to inclusive practices. For example, inquire about their experience handling situations involving potential discrimination or bias. This demonstrates your awareness and sends a clear message that you are seeking an agent who will actively champion your interests. You might also inquire about their knowledge of local resources and support networks that cater to the LGBTQ+ community.

Furthermore, consider asking about their familiarity with specific legal and financial considerations relevant to LGBTQ+ couples. Same-sex couples, for example, may face unique legal challenges related to property ownership, inheritance, and tax implications. A knowledgeable agent will be aware of these complexities and have the expertise or resources to navigate them effectively. Inquire about their understanding of these matters and how they can support you through these legal nuances. Their response will reveal their level of preparation and commitment to protecting your best interests. Transparency is essential, and a reputable agent should readily answer your questions and address your concerns without hesitation.

It's also crucial to assess the agent's communication style and responsiveness. A strong working relationship with your agent is vital throughout the home-buying process. You need someone who is readily available, responsive to your inquiries, and willing to proactively address any issues that may arise. An agent’s responsiveness reflects their commitment to providing excellent service and prioritizing your needs. A lack of responsiveness could indicate a potential lack of commitment to representing your interests effectively.

Beyond technical skills and qualifications, consider the personal connection you develop with the agent. The home- buying process can be emotionally taxing, so selecting an agent with whom you feel comfortable and trust is paramount. Choose someone who listens attentively to your needs, understands your priorities, and makes you feel respected and valued. A strong rapport and mutual trust contribute significantly to a positive and successful experience.

Remember, you’re entrusting this agent with one of the most significant financial and emotional decisions of your life, so it's crucial to find someone you connect with on a personal level and have complete confidence in their abilities.

Beyond simply finding an agent who identifies as LGBTQ+ or supports the community, it’s also critical to ensure they have a strong track record and expertise in the real estate market in your chosen area. A good agent will have an intimate understanding of the local market, including pricing trends, neighborhood dynamics, and potential challenges. This understanding is crucial in helping you find a property that meets your needs and budget. Don’t hesitate to ask for references and reviews from past clients, and if possible, speak with those clients directly to gauge their experiences. Checking online reviews and ratings can also provide valuable insights into the agent's professionalism, responsiveness, and overall client satisfaction.

Remember that you have a right to fair and equal treatment throughout the home-buying process. The Fair Housing Act protects against discrimination based on race, color, national origin, religion, sex, familial status, or disability. While sexual orientation and gender identity are not explicitly included in the act, many states and localities have expanded protections to include these characteristics. If you encounter any form of discrimination or bias, document the instance, and promptly report it to the appropriate authorities. Your real estate agent, being well-versed in these protections, should be able to assist you in navigating such situations and provide support if needed.

Once you've identified a few promising candidates, don't hesitate to ask about their fees and commission structures. Understanding these costs upfront is crucial to avoid surprises during the transaction. While commission rates are often standardized within a given region, ensure you understand all associated costs and whether additional fees are applied. An open discussion about fees ensures transparency and prevents any potential financial misunderstandings.

Ultimately, finding the right LGBTQ+-friendly real estate agent is a process of careful consideration, due diligence, and establishing a strong personal connection. Don't rush the process. Take the time to interview several agents, ask probing questions, and assess not only their professional qualifications but also their personal commitment to inclusivity and their understanding of your unique needs as a member of the LGBTQ+ community. This investment in due diligence will pay off handsomely by ensuring a positive, supportive, and successful home-buying experience. Remember, finding the right agent is as much about building a relationship as it is about finding someone with the necessary expertise. This crucial relationship will help guide you through one of the most significant financial and emotional steps of your life.

Protecting Yourself From Housing Discrimination

Finding the right real estate agent is only the first step in securing a home. The next, and perhaps more challenging, hurdle is navigating the potential for housing discrimination. While the Fair Housing Act of 1968 prohibits discrimination based on race, color, national origin, religion, sex, familial status, and disability, it notably does not explicitly include sexual orientation or gender identity. This omission leaves LGBTQ+ individuals and couples particularly vulnerable to discriminatory practices in the housing market. However, many states and localities have enacted their own fair housing laws that do offer broader protection, including explicit coverage for sexual orientation and gender identity. Understanding your rights and knowing how to protect yourself is crucial.

One common form of discrimination is refusal to rent or sell. This can manifest subtly or overtly. A landlord might claim an apartment is unavailable when it isn't, or an agent might steer you towards properties in less desirable neighborhoods, subtly implying that your presence wouldn't be welcome in more affluent areas. Real estate agents, even those professing LGBTQ+ friendliness, may subconsciously perpetuate these biases if not actively trained to combat them. This makes choosing an agent with explicit training in fair housing practices—even if they do not explicitly serve the LGBTQ+ community—a crucial decision.

Another insidious form of discrimination involves different terms or conditions. This could involve charging higher rents or deposits, imposing stricter application requirements, or delaying the approval process compared to other prospective tenants or buyers. For example, a same-sex couple might find themselves facing more stringent credit checks or being asked for significantly larger security deposits than heterosexual couples with comparable financial backgrounds. These practices, while not outright refusals, constitute discriminatory actions under fair housing laws where applicable. Documentation is paramount in these instances. Keep detailed records of all communication, including emails, text messages, and notes from phone conversations.

Discriminatory advertising is another area of concern. Advertisements that explicitly exclude LGBTQ+ individuals or subtly suggest that only certain types of people are welcome are illegal in jurisdictions with inclusive fair housing laws. Examples of such advertising include using language that evokes traditional family structures or excluding imagery that depicts diverse families. Even a seemingly innocuous phrase, if interpreted within context as exclusionary, can be grounds for a complaint. It is advisable to report such instances to the appropriate authorities and potentially engage an attorney who specializes in housing discrimination cases.

Beyond overt actions, subtle biases can be equally damaging. These can take the form of dismissive behavior, lack of responsiveness, or a general sense of being unwelcome. For instance, an agent might spend less time showing properties to LGBTQ+ couples or fail to answer their questions thoroughly compared to heterosexual clients. While proving these subtle biases is legally complex, diligent documentation can be beneficial. Record the length of interactions, note any dismissive or evasive answers, and keep a detailed log of every interaction.

In protecting yourself, several steps can significantly mitigate the risk of experiencing housing discrimination:

Know Your Rights: Research the fair housing laws in your state and locality. Understand what constitutes discrimination and what legal recourse is available to you. Many LGBTQ+ legal organizations provide valuable resources and guidance.

Documentation is Key: Document everything. Keep copies of all communications, including emails, text messages, letters, and notes from conversations. Note the date, time, and any specifics of interactions where you sensed discrimination. Even if you cannot fully prove your case in court, a robust record of your experience demonstrates good-faith efforts to seek redress.

Choose Your Words Carefully: While you have a right to disclose your sexual orientation or gender identity, consider the context. If you are uncomfortable disclosing this information upfront, it is not legally required in most jurisdictions, particularly in initial conversations with potential landlords or agents.

Find an Ally: If possible, have a friend or family member accompany you during property viewings or meetings with landlords or real estate agents. A witness to potentially discriminatory behavior can strengthen your position if you need to file a complaint.

Consider Legal Counsel: If you believe you have been a victim of housing discrimination, consult an attorney specializing in fair housing or LGBTQ+ rights. They can advise you on the best course of action and represent you in legal proceedings if necessary.

Report Discrimination: Report instances of suspected discrimination to the appropriate authorities. This might include your state's fair housing agency, the Department of Housing and Urban Development (HUD), or local human rights commissions. Each agency has a process for filing complaints and investigating claims of discrimination.

Use Anonymous Reporting: Many reporting systems allow for anonymous reporting, meaning you can report your experience without needing to disclose your identity if you feel uncomfortable doing so.

Navigating the housing market as an LGBTQ+ individual or couple requires vigilance and proactive measures. While the legal protections vary depending on your location, understanding your rights and how to document potential discriminatory practices are crucial steps in ensuring a fair and equitable experience. Remember that seeking legal counsel early can be invaluable in navigating complex situations and protecting your rights. With proactive measures and a clear understanding of your legal protections, you can significantly improve your chances of finding safe, inclusive, and welcoming housing

Building Wealth Through Home Ownership

Building wealth is a cornerstone of financial security, and for LGBTQ+ individuals, it often carries added significance, serving as a crucial step towards achieving economic independence and resilience against systemic inequalities. Homeownership presents a powerful avenue for wealth accumulation, offering a unique opportunity to build equity and generate long-term financial growth. However, the path to homeownership for LGBTQ+ individuals and couples isn't always straightforward, necessitating a nuanced understanding of the market and the potential challenges.

One of the most significant benefits of homeownership lies in its potential for equity growth. Equity represents the portion of your home's value that you own outright, representing the difference between your home’s market value and the outstanding mortgage balance. As your home appreciates in value, so does your equity. This appreciation acts as a tangible asset that grows over time, providing a financial safety net and a valuable foundation for future investments. This is fundamentally different from renting, where your monthly payments contribute directly to the landlord's wealth accumulation, not yours.

Beyond the appreciation, the consistent and predictable monthly mortgage payments contribute significantly to building equity. Every payment you make reduces the principal balance, increasing your ownership stake in your home. While interest payments initially represent a significant portion of your mortgage payment, the percentage of principal paid increases over the life of the loan, leading to a gradual yet substantial increase in equity. This consistent buildup of equity is a powerful long-term investment strategy, particularly crucial for those aiming for financial independence.

Moreover, homeownership offers significant tax advantages. In many jurisdictions, mortgage interest and property taxes are deductible, reducing your overall tax burden. These deductions can be substantial, effectively lowering the cost of your housing and freeing up more disposable income for other financial goals, like retirement savings or investments. It's vital to consult with a tax professional to fully understand the implications of these deductions and how they might impact your overall financial plan, as tax laws can vary significantly.

Beyond the financial benefits, homeownership provides a sense of security and stability that extends beyond the purely monetary. Owning your home provides a sense of permanence and control over your living environment, something particularly valuable for LGBTQ+ individuals who may have experienced instability or discrimination in the rental market. Knowing you have a safe, stable place to call home fosters a sense of belonging and well-being, fostering both mental and emotional stability. This sense of security is invaluable, transcending the purely financial aspects of homeownership.

However, the path to homeownership is not without its potential obstacles, particularly for LGBTQ+ individuals. Access to mortgage financing can be particularly challenging. While overt discrimination is illegal, subtle biases can still exist within lending institutions, leading to higher interest rates or stricter lending criteria for LGBTQ+ applicants. Furthermore, the historical and ongoing systemic inequalities that impact the LGBTQ+ community may result in lower credit scores or less access to financial resources, creating additional barriers to securing a mortgage.

It's therefore essential for LGBTQ+ individuals seeking to become homeowners to proactively address these potential challenges. Thorough financial planning is paramount. This includes diligently building and maintaining a strong credit score, saving diligently for a down payment, and carefully budgeting to ensure affordability. Working with a financial advisor experienced in LGBTQ+ financial planning can be incredibly beneficial in navigating these complexities, providing personalized guidance and tailored strategies to overcome potential hurdles.

Moreover, choosing the right real estate agent is a crucial decision. Finding an agent who is not only knowledgeable but also actively committed to fair housing practices is vital. An agent sensitive to the unique challenges faced by LGBTQ+ individuals can provide invaluable support and advocacy throughout the home-buying process, ensuring that you have an equitable and positive experience. Don't hesitate to interview several agents before making a decision, focusing on their experience, understanding of fair housing laws, and commitment to inclusivity.

Beyond the financial aspects, carefully consider the legal protections available in your area regarding fair housing practices. While federal law prohibits discrimination based on several factors, sexual orientation and gender identity are not explicitly included in all jurisdictions. Understanding your local laws, and the specific protections they offer, is critical in mitigating potential risks of discriminatory practices. Knowing your rights, and how to document any potential instances of discrimination provides an essential layer of protection.

In addition to finding the right agent, it is also wise to

carefully select a mortgage lender committed to inclusive lending practices. Just as with real estate agents, interview different lenders, inquiring about their commitment to fair lending and their understanding of the unique needs of LGBTQ+ clients. Ensure they have a robust understanding of fair housing laws and a proven track record of serving diverse communities.

Throughout the home-buying process, meticulous documentation is essential. Keep meticulous records of all communication, including emails, text messages, phone calls, and any written agreements. This documentation serves as a critical protection against potential disputes or instances of discrimination. Detailed records can be invaluable in demonstrating good-faith efforts, even if it becomes necessary to seek legal recourse.

The benefits of homeownership extend far beyond simply having a roof over your head; it is a crucial step in building long-term financial stability and security. For LGBTQ+ individuals and couples, the significance of homeownership is often amplified due to systemic challenges and historical disparities. By taking proactive steps, educating yourself on the process, and choosing the right professionals to work with, you can confidently navigate the path to homeownership, building a foundation for financial independence and a secure future. This process is a journey of empowerment, strengthening financial resilience and contributing to the long-term prosperity of the LGBTQ+ community. Remember, building equity is a process, and the rewards of this significant step are worth the effort and careful planning involved. The journey to homeownership should be empowering, and the resulting financial security a source of strength and pride.

Managing Home Ownership Expenses

Managing the ongoing costs associated with homeownership is crucial for long-term financial success. While the initial purchase price and mortgage payments are significant, they represent only a portion of the total financial commitment. Unexpected repairs, fluctuating property taxes, and insurance premiums can significantly impact your budget if not properly planned for. This section will guide you through the various expenses, providing strategies for budgeting and mitigating potential financial surprises.

Property taxes are a significant annual expense for homeowners. These taxes fund essential local services, including schools, public safety, and infrastructure. The amount you pay depends on the assessed value of your property and the local tax rate, which can vary considerably depending on your location. It's essential to understand your local tax rates and the assessed value of your property before purchasing a home. Many jurisdictions allow you to access your property's assessed value online, often through the county assessor's website. Understanding this number allows you to accurately budget for property taxes and factor them into your overall monthly expenses. Some mortgage lenders include property tax payments in your escrow account, making payments automatic and simplifying budgeting. However, even with escrow, it's still critical to understand the underlying tax rate and how it could fluctuate in the future. Property tax reassessments are common, and understanding the process in your area will allow you to anticipate and adjust your budget accordingly. If you are unsure, seeking advice from a financial professional or tax advisor specializing in real estate can prove invaluable.

Homeowners insurance is another non-negotiable expense. This policy protects your investment and provides financial coverage in the event of damage or loss to your property. The cost of homeowners insurance varies widely, influenced by several factors, including the location of your home, the age and condition of the property, the coverage amount, and your deductible. Factors like your credit score can even impact your insurance premiums, reinforcing the importance of credit health. When comparing insurance policies, carefully review the coverage details and compare premiums from multiple insurers to ensure you're getting the best value for your needs. Working with an independent insurance agent can provide access to a wider range of options and help you navigate the complexities of insurance policies. Don't hesitate to ask questions; understanding your coverage is essential in mitigating potential financial risks.

Beyond property taxes and insurance, you must budget for regular maintenance and potential repairs. Owning a home involves ongoing responsibilities. Regular maintenance, such as cleaning gutters, inspecting appliances, and performing routine upkeep, can prevent larger, more expensive problems down the line. An ounce of prevention is worth a pound of cure. Scheduling annual inspections and addressing minor issues promptly can significantly reduce the likelihood of costly repairs. Creating a maintenance schedule and setting aside funds for these expenses is crucial for responsible homeownership. This includes creating a plan for larger repairs that might arise, such as a new roof or HVAC system replacement. These unforeseen costs, while unpredictable, are a normal part of homeownership and require planning. Consider establishing a dedicated savings account specifically for home repairs and maintenance, allowing for consistent contributions to address unexpected issues without disrupting your overall financial plan.

Unexpected repairs are a common cost of homeownership that often catches homeowners off guard. A sudden plumbing issue, a malfunctioning appliance, or storm damage can all generate substantial expenses. Creating an emergency fund specifically for home repairs is therefore essential. This fund serves as a safety net, providing a financial cushion when unforeseen issues arise. This fund should be separate from your general emergency fund and ideally large enough to cover several thousand dollars in repair costs. Having this financial protection can prevent unexpected expenses from causing financial stress and potential debt. Regularly review and adjust your emergency fund based on your home's age and potential risks. Older homes may require a larger emergency fund due to the increased probability of repairs. Similarly, homes in areas prone to natural disasters may require additional savings to cover potential damage.

Beyond these core expenses, additional costs can arise. These include homeowner association (HOA) fees, if applicable, landscaping costs, and utility bills. HOA fees cover the maintenance of common areas in your community. Landscaping can range from simple lawn care to professional gardening services. Utility bills, including electricity, water, gas, and internet, vary depending on usage and local rates. Accurately budgeting for these expenses is crucial, and you might consider tracking your utility usage for several months before purchasing a home to get a better understanding of expected costs.

Managing these expenses effectively requires diligent budgeting and financial planning. A comprehensive budget that allocates funds for each expense is crucial. Consider using budgeting software or apps to track your income and expenses. This will help you identify areas where you might reduce spending and ensure sufficient funds are allocated to homeownership costs.

Regularly reviewing and adjusting your budget as needed is vital, especially when facing unexpected expenses or changes in your financial situation. Consider consulting a financial advisor who specializes in LGBTQ+ financial planning. They can help you develop a personalized budget tailored to your circumstances, ensuring you're prepared for the financial responsibilities of homeownership Furthermore, it's wise to have a clear understanding of your homeowner's insurance policy. Know precisely what is covered, what your deductible is, and what steps to take in case of damage or loss. A thorough review of your policy, preferably annually, will ensure you understand your rights and responsibilities. In the case of a major repair, understand your policy's coverage and the process for filing a claim. Proactive planning and a detailed understanding of your insurance coverage will make managing unexpected repairs significantly less stressful.

Homeownership comes with significant financial responsibilities, but effective management of these expenses ensures long-term financial health and security. By proactively budgeting for property taxes, insurance, maintenance, and other related costs, you can safeguard your investment and avoid potential financial difficulties. Remember, building equity in your home is a marathon, not a sprint. Careful planning, consistent budgeting, and regular review of your financial situation will ensure your journey toward homeownership remains a path of empowerment and stability. The long-term benefits of homeownership, including financial security and a sense of belonging, are worth the ongoing effort and planning involved. Remember to leverage the resources available, such as financial advisors specializing in LGBTQ+ needs, to navigate this significant life step successfully.

6

EDUCATION AND CAREER PLANNING: INVESTING IN YOUR FUTURE

Funding Higher Education Scholarship And Financial Aid

Funding higher education can feel daunting, especially when navigating the complexities of financial aid and scholarships. However, with careful planning and research, accessing the resources available to LGBTQ+ students can significantly ease the burden. This section will equip you with the knowledge and strategies to secure the funding you need to pursue your educational goals.

The journey to securing financial aid often begins with

completing the Free Application for Federal Student Aid (FAFSA). This crucial form determines your eligibility for federal grants, loans, and work-study programs. The FAFSA is a gateway to a variety of federal aid options designed to assist students of all backgrounds, including LGBTQ+ individuals. Understanding the process and deadlines is paramount; missing deadlines can jeopardize your chances of receiving timely aid. Be sure to complete the FAFSA as early as possible, typically opening in October of each year for the following academic year.

While the FAFSA is a cornerstone of the financial aid process, it’s essential to remember it's not the only resource available. Many state-level financial aid programs also exist, offering additional grants and scholarships tailored to specific state residents. Research your state’s higher education website to uncover these opportunities. These state-specific programs often have additional requirements or criteria for eligibility, so thoroughly review the details to ensure you meet all qualifications. State aid programs can vary significantly from state to state, so your research must be location-specific. This further underscores the importance of early planning and diligent research.

Beyond federal and state resources, a wealth of private scholarships and grants are specifically geared towards LGBTQ+ students. Numerous organizations and foundations dedicate themselves to supporting LGBTQ+ individuals in their pursuit of higher education. These scholarships often recognize not only academic achievement but also community involvement, leadership qualities, and commitment to LGBTQ+ advocacy. Some organizations offer scholarships based on specific academic majors or career interests. For example, there are scholarships specifically for students pursuing careers in medicine, law, engineering, or the arts. Finding the right scholarship requires thorough research.

Your research strategy should involve a multi-pronged approach. Start by exploring the websites of LGBTQ+ organizations, such as The Trevor Project, GLAAD, and the Human Rights Campaign. Many of these organizations maintain comprehensive scholarship databases, providing a centralized resource for LGBTQ+ students searching for funding. The websites often include detailed eligibility criteria, application deadlines, and contact information for scholarship providers. Many LGBTQ+ community centers and local organizations can also provide valuable guidance and resources in your area.

In addition to national organizations, many colleges and universities offer scholarships specifically for LGBTQ+ students. Check with the financial aid or scholarship offices of the colleges and universities to which you are applying. These institutional scholarships can be highly competitive, so ensure your application materials—including essays, transcripts, and letters of recommendation—are of the highest quality. Strong application materials demonstrate your commitment to your education and your ability to excel academically.

When searching for scholarships, carefully review the eligibility requirements for each award. Some scholarships may have specific GPA requirements, while others may prioritize students from certain backgrounds or with particular academic interests. Many scholarships also require essays or personal statements, providing an opportunity to share your unique experiences and perspectives. These essays are critical; they give you the chance to illustrate your commitment to your education and your passion for your chosen field. Craft compelling narratives that highlight your personal achievements and aspirations.

Remember that the application process for scholarships can be time-consuming. Set aside ample time to carefully review each scholarship opportunity and prepare complete and accurate application materials. Keep a calendar or spreadsheet to track application deadlines and ensure you submit everything on time. Missing a deadline can eliminate your chances for funding, so organization and time management are paramount.

Beyond scholarships, exploring grants is another crucial avenue for securing funding. Grants, like scholarships, are forms of financial aid that do not need to be repaid. Unlike loans, grants don't create future debt obligations. However, securing grants can be equally competitive and often requires meticulous research. Explore grant opportunities from national foundations, philanthropic organizations, and local community groups. Many grants are focused on specific areas of study or support students with particular needs.

Financial aid for higher education isn't just about scholarships and grants; federal student loans are also an option for covering educational expenses. While loans require repayment, they can bridge the gap between the cost of education and other financial aid received. Understand the terms and conditions of different loan types, including interest rates, repayment plans, and potential consequences of default. Explore federal student loan options before turning to private lenders, as federal loans often have more favorable terms and repayment options.

When considering student loans, it's crucial to borrow only what is necessary to avoid overwhelming debt. Carefully assess your financial situation, and create a realistic budget that accounts for tuition, fees, housing, and living expenses. Explore work-study opportunities available at your institution to supplement your financial aid and reduce your reliance on loans. Part-time employment can significantly impact your financial picture during your college years.

As you navigate the complexities of financial aid, don't

hesitate to seek professional guidance. Many colleges and universities have financial aid offices staffed with experienced counselors who can provide personalized advice and support. They can assist you in completing the FAFSA, exploring available scholarships, and understanding loan options. Moreover, seek advice from a financial advisor who specializes in LGBTQ+ financial planning. They can offer tailored guidance specific to your circumstances and provide valuable insights into financial management during and after your education.

The pursuit of higher education is an investment in your future. Securing the necessary funding requires diligent research, careful planning, and proactive engagement with available resources. By utilizing the resources discussed in this section, you can significantly increase your chances of obtaining the financial support you need to pursue your educational goals and achieve your full potential. Remember that financial aid is not just about the money; it's about creating a path to your dreams and securing a brighter future. Embrace the challenge, persevere through the process, and celebrate your accomplishments along the way.

The journey to financial security and educational attainment is achievable with careful planning and the utilization of available resources.

Career Planning and Financial Stability

Building a fulfilling and financially secure career is a crucial component of long-term financial well-being, particularly for LGBTQ+ individuals who may face unique challenges in the professional world. This section explores strategies for identifying high-paying career paths, navigating potential workplace discrimination, and building financial stability throughout your career.

One of the first steps involves identifying careers that align with your interests and skills while also offering strong earning potential. While passion is essential, it's equally crucial to consider the financial realities of different career paths. Researching salary data for various occupations can provide valuable insights into potential earnings. Resources like the Bureau of Labor Statistics (BLS) offer comprehensive salary information broken down by occupation, location, and experience level. Pay attention to projected job growth; choosing a career field with strong growth potential can enhance your long-term earning potential and job security.

However, simply focusing on high-paying careers isn't sufficient. Consider the work-life balance offered by different professions. Some high-paying jobs demand long hours and significant dedication, potentially impacting personal well- being.

Carefully weigh the financial benefits against the potential costs to your personal life. A balanced approach that prioritizes both financial security and personal fulfillment is essential for sustainable well-being.

The LGBTQ+ community often faces unique challenges in the professional world, including discrimination and bias. While legal protections exist in many areas, subtle forms of discrimination can still hinder career advancement. Networking within the LGBTQ+ community can provide valuable support and access to mentorship opportunities. Joining professional organizations with LGBTQ+ inclusivity initiatives can connect you with like-minded professionals and potential allies within your chosen field. These networks offer invaluable support and can open doors to opportunities otherwise inaccessible.

Furthermore, cultivating strong professional skills and building a strong work ethic are essential for career success. Focus on developing skills that are in high demand in your chosen field. Consider pursuing advanced certifications, professional development courses, or even further education to enhance your marketability and earning potential. Continuous learning is not just about acquiring new skills; it's also about showcasing your commitment to professional growth and your adaptability in a constantly evolving job market.

When it comes to securing employment, crafting a compelling resume and cover letter is paramount. Highlight your accomplishments, skills, and experiences in a way that demonstrates your value to potential employers. Tailor your resume and cover letter to each specific job application, showcasing how your skills and experiences directly align with the employer's requirements. Consider seeking assistance from career counselors or professional resume writers, particularly if you're facing challenges showcasing your skills effectively.

The interview process also holds significant weight. Practice your interviewing skills, and prepare thoughtful answers to common interview questions. Research the company and the interviewers beforehand, demonstrating your genuine interest in the position and the organization. Presenting yourself confidently and professionally during the interview is critical to making a strong first impression.

Once employed, building strong relationships with your colleagues and superiors is crucial for career advancement. Collaborate effectively with your team, take initiative on projects, and demonstrate your commitment to your work. Actively seeking feedback and utilizing it to improve your performance is also essential for professional growth. Remember that building a positive professional reputation within your workplace can significantly contribute to career progression.

Beyond your immediate workplace, active networking outside your company can enhance your career trajectory. Attend industry conferences, join professional organizations, and participate in networking events. These activities provide opportunities to expand your professional network, learn about new opportunities, and potentially secure mentorship or sponsorship from senior professionals.

Financial stability requires careful planning and consistent effort. Create a realistic budget that accounts for all expenses, including housing, transportation, food, and debt payments. Tracking your income and expenses can help you identify areas where you can cut back and save money. Explore different savings strategies, such as setting up an emergency fund, contributing to a retirement account, and investing in other financial instruments.

For LGBTQ+ individuals, planning for potential healthcare expenses is crucial, considering the potential higher cost of healthcare and access barriers faced by the community. A robust healthcare plan with comprehensive coverage is essential. Research the different options available, and choose a plan that meets your individual needs and budget.

Building financial security also necessitates understanding and managing debt. Minimize high-interest debt like credit card debt, prioritize paying off high-interest debts first, and explore options for debt consolidation or refinancing. Develop a strategy for managing your debt effectively, and seek professional advice if necessary.

Regularly reviewing and adjusting your financial plan is essential. Life circumstances can change unexpectedly, requiring adjustments to your budget and financial goals. Regularly reassessing your financial position, incorporating any changes in income or expenses, ensures your financial plan remains aligned with your evolving needs. Consider working with a financial advisor specializing in LGBTQ+ financial planning, who can provide personalized guidance tailored to your unique circumstances.

In summary, building a thriving career and securing financial stability requires proactive planning, consistent effort, and a willingness to adapt to the ever-evolving landscape of the professional world. By combining passion with a pragmatic approach to career planning, financial management, and networking, LGBTQ+ individuals can achieve long-term financial success and create a secure and fulfilling future. Remember to leverage the resources available to the LGBTQ+ community and seek professional guidance when needed. The journey may have its challenges, but with careful planning and perseverance, it is a journey worth undertaking.]

Negotiating Salary and Benefits

Negotiating salary and benefits can feel daunting, especially when you're starting your career or changing jobs. However, it's a crucial skill for building long-term financial security, particularly within the LGBTQ+ community where fair compensation isn't always guaranteed. This isn't just about securing a higher paycheck; it's about advocating for your worth and ensuring you receive the support you need to thrive.

Before you even step into a salary negotiation, thorough research is essential. Understand the market value of your skills and experience in your field and location. Utilize online resources like Glassdoor, Salary.com, Payscale, and the Bureau of Labor Statistics to gather salary data for similar roles. Pay close attention to factors like education level, years of experience, and company size, as these significantly influence compensation packages. Don't just focus on the average salary; look at the range to get a realistic understanding of what's possible.

Consider your unique skills and experiences. Do you possess specialized certifications, advanced degrees, or unique skills that are highly sought after in your industry? If so, these should be highlighted during the negotiation process. Quantify your achievements whenever possible. Instead of simply stating you "improved efficiency," explain how you "increased efficiency by

15%, resulting in a $X cost savings for the company." This demonstrates the tangible value you bring to the table.

Networking plays a crucial role in salary negotiation. Talking to colleagues, mentors, and other professionals in your field can provide invaluable insights into typical salary ranges and negotiation strategies. Leverage your LGBTQ+ networks; these connections can offer unique perspectives and support during the process. Sharing experiences with others who have navigated similar negotiations can empower you and reduce feelings of anxiety.

Prepare a comprehensive list of your desired compensation and benefits. Don't just focus on your salary; consider the overall package. Benefits such as health insurance, retirement plans, paid time off, parental leave, and professional development opportunities are all significant components of your total compensation. Research the benefits offered by the company and the industry standards, making sure to advocate for comprehensive benefits that meet your individual needs. For LGBTQ+ individuals, this is particularly important, as access to inclusive healthcare and benefits can significantly impact financial well-being.

During the negotiation process, present your value proposition confidently and professionally. Start by expressing your enthusiasm for the role and the company. Then, clearly and concisely state your salary expectations, basing them on your research and the value you bring. Be prepared to justify your request, highlighting your skills, experience, and accomplishments. Remember that it's acceptable to negotiate; don't be afraid to counter-offer if the initial offer is below your expectations. Negotiation is a two- way street, and a successful outcome requires mutual respect and understanding.

Practice your negotiation skills beforehand. Role-playing with a trusted friend or mentor can help you build confidence and refine your approach. Consider different scenarios and potential responses from the employer, preparing yourself for a range of outcomes. Understanding potential counterarguments and having well-thought-out responses will demonstrate your preparedness and professionalism.

If the company presents a counteroffer that doesn't meet your expectations, don't be afraid to walk away. While it's tempting to accept the first offer, especially if you're eager for a new position, remember that your worth should be reflected in your compensation. Walking away demonstrates confidence in your value and your commitment to securing a fair compensation package. It might also incentivize the employer to reconsider their offer.

Remember that you're not just negotiating a salary; you're negotiating a future. A fair compensation package allows you to build financial stability, invest in your future, and enjoy a higher quality of life. For LGBTQ+ individuals, securing a financially secure future is particularly crucial, given the potential for discrimination and challenges in accessing resources. This negotiation is an investment in your well- being, both financially and emotionally.

Don't underestimate the power of understanding the company's financial position. While focusing on your value, understanding the company's budget and financial constraints can help you tailor your negotiation strategy. This doesn't mean accepting a lower offer than you deserve, but it shows your professionalism and consideration. For example, if the company is facing financial challenges, proposing a slightly lower salary in exchange for additional benefits or a faster career progression could be a viable alternative.

Consider the long-term implications of your salary negotiation. Don't just focus on the immediate financial benefits; consider the impact on your future earning potential. A higher starting salary can set you on a path to higher earnings throughout your career, leading to greater financial security in the long run. It's also beneficial to negotiate for professional development opportunities that will enhance your skills and increase your earning potential in the future.

Once you've secured a job offer, review the entire package carefully. Understand all the terms and conditions, including salary, benefits, bonuses, and any other incentives. Don't hesitate to ask clarifying questions if anything is unclear. If you're unsure about any aspect of the package, seek advice from a trusted financial advisor or legal professional who specializes in LGBTQ+ financial planning. They can provide invaluable guidance in ensuring you're making the right decision.

Beyond the initial negotiation, remain proactive in advocating for your needs throughout your career. Regularly review your compensation and benefits, ensuring they remain competitive with the market. Seek feedback from your superiors and colleagues to identify areas where you can improve your performance and justify further salary increases. Continuous professional development and advancement showcase your dedication and increase your worth within the company, strengthening your position for future negotiations.

In conclusion, negotiating salary and benefits is an essential skill for LGBTQ+ individuals seeking financial security and career advancement. By conducting thorough research, building strong networks, preparing a comprehensive strategy, and advocating for your worth, you can achieve a compensation package that reflects your value and sets you on a path to long-term financial success. Remember that your financial well-being is paramount, and advocating for yourself is a vital step in achieving it. Don't be afraid to ask for what you deserve; your financial future depends on it. The process may be challenging, but the rewards are well worth the effort. Remember to seek professional support when needed, and celebrate your successes along the way. This is a crucial step towards building a financially secure and fulfilling future. Your worth is undeniable, and your ability to advocate for yourself is empowering.

Building A Strong Professional Network

Building a strong professional network is paramount for career advancement and financial success, especially within the LGBTQ+ community. While navigating the professional world, LGBTQ+ individuals may face unique challenges, including potential discrimination and a lack of visible role models. Therefore, cultivating a supportive and expansive network is not simply beneficial, it's essential for securing opportunities and advocating for fair treatment. This network serves as a source of mentorship, support, and access to hidden job markets and opportunities that may not be advertised publicly.

The first step in building a robust professional network involves actively seeking out opportunities for connection. This goes beyond simply attending industry events; it requires a strategic and proactive approach. Consider joining professional organizations relevant to your field. Many professional associations have LGBTQ+ employee resource groups (ERGs) or affinity groups that provide a safe and supportive space to network with like-minded individuals. These groups often host events, workshops, and networking opportunities tailored to the specific needs and interests of LGBTQ+ professionals. Participating in these events allows you to build relationships with individuals who understand the unique challenges and triumphs of navigating a career while being part of the LGBTQ+ community.

Beyond formal organizations, leverage online platforms like LinkedIn to connect with professionals in your field. Join relevant groups, participate in discussions, and actively engage with others' posts. LinkedIn provides a powerful platform to showcase your skills and experience, and to make meaningful connections with people you might not otherwise encounter. Remember to personalize your LinkedIn profile, highlighting your accomplishments and emphasizing your commitment to diversity and inclusion. This will make your profile more visible and attractive to potential connections within the LGBTQ+ community and beyond.

Networking isn't just about collecting business cards; it’s about building genuine relationships. Focus on fostering meaningful connections with individuals who share your professional goals and values, regardless of their background or identity. Engage in conversations, offer assistance when appropriate, and genuinely seek to learn from others' experiences. These authentic interactions are more likely to lead to long-term professional relationships that can benefit your career trajectory.

Attend industry conferences and workshops. These events provide valuable opportunities to meet professionals from various companies and backgrounds. Take advantage of networking sessions, lunch breaks, and informal gatherings to connect with people. Prepare a concise and engaging introduction that highlights your professional background and interests. Remember to actively listen during conversations and show genuine interest in the other person's work. Don't be afraid to initiate conversations, even with individuals you might perceive as being more senior or established in their careers.

Mentorship plays a crucial role in professional development and networking. Seeking out a mentor who can provide guidance, support, and advocacy can greatly enhance your career progression. Mentors can offer invaluable advice on navigating workplace dynamics, building your skills, and securing promotions. If possible, seek a mentor within the LGBTQ+ community who understands the specific challenges and opportunities you may face. Many organizations offer mentorship programs specifically for LGBTQ+ professionals, connecting mentees with experienced professionals who can provide support and guidance. If a formal mentorship program isn't available, consider reaching out to individuals you admire within your network and express your interest in seeking their mentorship.

Mentorship is a two-way street; consider offering mentorship to others as well. Sharing your knowledge and experiences with junior colleagues can not only help them succeed but also strengthen your own network and leadership skills. Mentoring others reinforces your professional expertise and builds your credibility within the industry.

Building a strong professional network requires consistent effort and engagement. Regularly attend networking events, stay active on professional platforms, and maintain contact with your connections. Sending a brief email to update them on your progress or inquire about their work can help sustain the relationships you've built. Remember to always be professional and respectful, regardless of the context. Your reputation and how you treat others is essential.

Don't limit your network to your immediate industry. Connecting with professionals in related fields can provide unexpected opportunities for collaboration and career advancement. Explore opportunities to expand your network through cross-industry events, workshops, and online groups. This broader perspective can help you identify new trends and opportunities that you might otherwise miss.

Leverage your existing network. Inform your friends, family, and former colleagues about your career goals and seek their assistance in expanding your professional connections. You never know where a valuable connection might lead. Ask them if they know anyone in your field or if they have any relevant industry contacts.

Remember that your network is an asset that requires nurturing and maintenance. Regularly check in with your contacts, offer support when possible, and celebrate their achievements. This will demonstrate your genuine interest in building and maintaining long-term relationships, fostering loyalty and mutual support within your professional circle. Reciprocity is key; be willing to help others as they may help you.

When networking, it is vital to be mindful of the unique challenges faced by LGBTQ+ individuals. Create a safe and inclusive space during interactions. Be mindful of the language you use and ensure you're creating an environment where everyone feels comfortable expressing themselves. Avoid making assumptions about someone’s identity or experience. If you are unsure about something, ask respectfully. This inclusive approach is crucial for building trust and establishing strong, lasting relationships within your network.

Networking is an ongoing process; it's not a one-time event but rather a continuous effort to cultivate and strengthen relationships. Be patient and persistent; building a strong network takes time and dedication. However, the rewards of a supportive professional network are immeasurable, providing access to opportunities, support, and a sense of community that is especially valuable for LGBTQ+ individuals navigating their careers. It's an investment in your future and your success. The effort you put into building and maintaining your network will significantly impact your career progression and financial security. Remember to celebrate milestones and acknowledge progress along the way. Building a powerful professional network is a crucial step towards building a successful and fulfilling career. It's about more than just career advancement; it's about building a community of support and creating a pathway to a future where you can thrive both personally and professionally. Investing in this aspect of your professional life is an investment in your overall well-being.

Managing Career Transitions and Financial Uncertainty

Navigating career transitions can be challenging for anyone, but LGBTQ+ individuals may face additional hurdles due to potential biases and discrimination. Job loss, whether voluntary or involuntary, often brings a wave of emotional and financial uncertainty. Understanding how to manage these transitions effectively is crucial for maintaining financial stability and well-being.

The first step is to acknowledge the emotional impact of a career change or job loss. Allow yourself time to process your feelings. Job loss can trigger feelings of anxiety, fear, anger, and even grief. These are normal reactions, and it's important to acknowledge them without judgment. Consider seeking support from friends, family, or a therapist. Many LGBTQ+-affirming therapists understand the unique challenges faced by our community and can provide valuable support during this difficult time. Support groups, either online or in-person, can also offer a sense of community and shared experience, allowing you to connect with others who understand what you're going through. Remember, you're not alone.

Once you've allowed yourself time to process your emotions, it's crucial to develop a comprehensive financial plan to address the immediate and long-term impacts of the change. This begins with assessing your current financial situation. Create a detailed budget that includes all income sources, expenses, and debt obligations. Understanding your financial landscape will help you determine your immediate needs and long-term goals. This might involve reducing expenses, exploring emergency funds, or seeking financial assistance.

Explore your savings and emergency funds. Ideally, you've built an emergency fund that can cover several months of living expenses. Accessing these funds can help alleviate immediate financial pressures. If your emergency fund is insufficient, explore options like borrowing from family or friends, obtaining a personal loan, or utilizing credit cards (responsibly). Be sure to consider the long-term implications of debt, and prioritize paying it down as quickly as possible.

Consider available financial assistance programs. Many governmental and non-governmental organizations offer financial aid to individuals facing job loss or financial hardship. These programs may provide unemployment benefits, food assistance, rental assistance, or other forms of support. Research local and national programs to determine your eligibility and access available resources. LGBTQ+- focused organizations often provide specialized assistance and support tailored to the needs of the community. They may offer financial counseling, job placement assistance, or other valuable services.

Review your insurance coverage. Unemployment insurance can provide temporary income during periods of joblessness. Health insurance is vital, and maintaining coverage should be a top priority. If you've lost your employer-sponsored health insurance, investigate options for obtaining individual or government-subsidized coverage through the Affordable Care Act (ACA) marketplace.

Begin actively searching for new employment opportunities. Update your resume and cover letter to highlight your skills and experience, emphasizing any relevant accomplishments and qualifications. Network actively within your professional circle, letting people know of your job search and skills. Leverage your previously built network, reaching out to former colleagues, mentors, and industry contacts. Consider consulting with a career coach, especially one with experience working with the LGBTQ+ community, who can provide guidance on refining your job search strategy and creating a competitive resume and cover letter.

Consider further education or skill development. If your previous role is no longer viable, or if you are interested in a career change, this is an opportunity to invest in your future. Explore professional development courses, online certifications, or educational programs that can enhance your skills and expand your career options. This can increase your marketability and open doors to new opportunities. Financial aid and scholarships may be available to assist with the costs of further education or training. Consider seeking advice from a financial advisor to determine the best path, balancing the cost of education with potential long-term earnings.

During periods of financial uncertainty, careful financial

management is paramount. Track your spending closely, reduce non-essential expenses, and explore ways to increase your income through freelancing, consulting, or part-time employment. Consider consulting with a financial advisor specializing in LGBTQ+ financial planning. They can provide personalized guidance on budgeting, debt management, and financial planning for various life stages. Many financial advisors offer free initial consultations, allowing you to discuss your specific financial situation and explore potential solutions.

If you're facing significant financial challenges, don't hesitate to seek professional help. Credit counseling agencies can offer guidance on managing debt and developing a plan for repayment. They can help negotiate with creditors to create more manageable payment plans and prevent defaults. These agencies can provide valuable assistance to individuals facing overwhelming debt. Remember, seeking professional help is a sign of strength, not weakness. It shows a proactive approach to managing your financial situation.

Career transitions and periods of financial uncertainty can be daunting. However, by proactively addressing the emotional and financial aspects of these challenges, you can build resilience and navigate these periods successfully. Remember to utilize available resources, build a supportive network, and seek professional help when needed. LGBTQ+ individuals have a unique set of skills and resilience. By investing in yourself and your future, you can emerge from these transitions stronger and more empowered. Your skills, talents, and resilience are valuable assets, regardless of the challenges you face. Remember to celebrate your achievements and acknowledge your resilience during this process.

Managing a career transition often requires adapting to new industries or skill sets. This can involve a period of self- reflection on your transferable skills and passions. For example, someone with a background in customer service could transition into roles in sales, teaching, or even human resources, leveraging their communication and interpersonal skills. Similarly, someone with analytical skills from a previous role could explore data analysis, research, or project management positions. Identifying your transferable skills is crucial for crafting a compelling narrative in your resume and cover letter, demonstrating your adaptability and value to prospective employers.

Consider seeking guidance from career counselors and mentors familiar with the LGBTQ+ community. These professionals can offer personalized support and advice, helping you identify and articulate your skills, create effective networking strategies, and navigate the job market confidently. Many organizations and community centers offer free or low-cost career services specifically for LGBTQ+ individuals. These resources often provide personalized support tailored to the unique needs and challenges faced by the community.

Building a strong support network is crucial during a career transition. Lean on trusted friends, family, and community members for emotional support and practical assistance. Connect with LGBTQ+ support groups or organizations where you can share your experiences, receive encouragement, and learn from others' journeys. These groups offer invaluable emotional support and a safe space to process emotions and anxieties associated with career transitions.

Beyond immediate financial concerns, consider the long-term implications of career changes on your financial planning. For instance, a significant career change might affect your retirement savings, social security benefits, and long-term financial stability. Consulting a financial planner familiar with LGBTQ+ issues can help you develop a comprehensive financial plan that takes into account these factors and ensures your long-term financial security. They can offer personalized strategies for saving, investing, and managing your finances to meet your individual needs and circumstances. This could involve reviewing your retirement savings strategy, exploring different investment options, and developing a plan to account for potential income fluctuations.

Remember to focus on self-care throughout the process. A career transition or financial uncertainty can be stressful. Prioritize your physical and mental health by engaging in activities that help you relax, such as exercise, meditation, or spending time in nature.

Maintaining a healthy lifestyle will improve your overall well-being and enhance your ability to cope with challenges. Ensure that you have strategies for managing stress and maintaining positive mental health. This could involve regular exercise, mindfulness practices, or seeking professional support from a therapist or counselor.

Navigating these transitions is a process requiring time, patience, and self-compassion. Celebrate small victories and acknowledge your resilience throughout the journey. You have valuable skills and experiences; your future is built on your strengths and adaptability. Remember to focus on your strengths and believe in your ability to overcome challenges. Your ability to navigate this transition is a testament to your strength and resilience.

7

GIVING BACK AND SUPPORTING THE COMMUNITY: PHILANTHROPY AND LEGACY

Charitable Giving and LGBTQ Organizations

Giving back to the community is a deeply rewarding act, and for LGBTQ+ individuals, it often holds a special significance. It's a chance to support the organizations and causes that have helped shape our lives and create a more inclusive and equitable future for generations to come. Charitable giving, whether through financial contributions, volunteering time, or in-kind donations, can be a powerful expression of our values and a way to leave a lasting legacy.

When considering charitable giving, many within the

LGBTQ+ community prioritize organizations that directly address issues relevant to our lives. These might include organizations focused on LGBTQ+ rights advocacy, HIV/AIDS research and support, mental health services for LGBTQ+ individuals, youth programs providing safe and affirming spaces, and organizations fighting against discrimination and violence. The range of causes is vast, reflecting the diversity within the LGBTQ+ community itself.

The decision of where to donate is deeply personal, and there is no right or wrong answer. Consider your own values and priorities. Are you passionate about supporting youth initiatives? Do you want to contribute to organizations working to combat HIV/AIDS? Or are you interested in organizations fighting for legislative change and equal rights? Identifying your passions will guide your choices and ensure your donations resonate with your personal values.

Before making a donation, research the organizations you are considering. Look for evidence of their effectiveness and transparency. Reputable organizations often provide detailed information on their programs, finances, and impact. Websites like Charity Navigator and GuideStar offer independent evaluations and ratings of charitable organizations, providing useful insights into their financial health and effectiveness. Don't hesitate to contact organizations directly to ask questions about their programs and how your donation will be used.

Beyond financial contributions, volunteering your time is another powerful way to support LGBTQ+ organizations. Many organizations rely on volunteers to provide critical support for their programs and services. Volunteering offers a chance to directly engage with the cause you care about, building deeper connections with the community and making a tangible impact. The roles available are as diverse as the organizations themselves. You might find yourself mentoring LGBTQ+ youth, assisting with fundraising events, providing administrative support, or even offering your professional skills to help with fundraising or marketing strategies.

Many LGBTQ+ organizations welcome in-kind donations, which can be just as valuable as financial contributions. Depending on the organization's needs, this might include office supplies, technology equipment, clothing, food, or even professional services. Donating in-kind gifts can be a practical way to support organizations with limited resources, ensuring they have the materials and support needed to carry out their mission. Consider what skills or resources you possess that could benefit a specific organization, and reach out to see if your contributions could be of use.

Estate planning offers a unique opportunity for long-term support of LGBTQ+ causes. Including charitable gifts in your will or establishing a charitable remainder trust allows you to leave a lasting legacy beyond your lifetime. These strategies can provide significant tax advantages while ensuring your cherished causes continue to receive support for years to come. It's wise to consult with an estate planning attorney specializing in LGBTQ+ issues to understand the various options available and to ensure your wishes are executed effectively. They can help navigate the complexities of estate planning, ensuring that your legacy aligns perfectly with your values and goals.

When planning your charitable giving, remember the importance of diversification. Donating to a variety of organizations working on different aspects of LGBTQ+ issues ensures a broader impact. Supporting both grassroots organizations with limited resources and larger, established organizations with extensive reach creates a balanced approach to your philanthropic endeavors. A well-rounded approach allows for support of different initiatives and maximizes your overall impact on the community.

For example, you might choose to donate to a local LGBTQ+ community center providing vital services, such as counseling, support groups, and youth programs. Simultaneously, you could contribute to a national organization advocating for legislative changes that affect the entire LGBTQ+ community. This balanced approach ensures support for both immediate needs and long-term systemic change, maximizing the positive impact of your charitable giving.

Building a sustainable philanthropic strategy is important for consistent giving. This could involve setting aside a specific amount each month or year for charitable donations, or even establishing a dedicated charitable giving account. Regular giving, even in smaller amounts, can add up over time and provide consistent support for the organizations you care about. Consistency allows organizations to plan their programs and allocate resources effectively, maximizing the impact of donations.

Consider the impact of your giving beyond the immediate financial contribution. Your donation might enable an organization to hire a crucial staff member, purchase much- needed equipment, or launch a new program addressing critical needs. Visualizing the positive impact of your donation can enhance the sense of fulfillment and satisfaction associated with charitable giving. Many organizations offer detailed reports showing the impact of donations, helping to illustrate how your contribution made a tangible difference.

Beyond monetary contributions, consider how your skills and expertise could benefit LGBTQ+ organizations. For instance, a financial advisor could offer pro bono financial planning services to LGBTQ+ youth or seniors, while a lawyer could provide legal assistance to those facing discrimination. Sharing your professional expertise can provide immense value to organizations that may have limited resources to access such services. This form of in- kind contribution adds significant value, often exceeding the monetary equivalent of the service provided.

Remember to seek professional advice when necessary. A financial advisor specializing in LGBTQ+ financial planning can assist with developing a comprehensive charitable giving strategy that aligns with your financial goals and philanthropic aspirations. They can help you explore tax- advantaged giving options and maximize the impact of your donations. Estate planning attorneys can advise on creating a legacy of giving through your will or trust, ensuring your wishes are carried out effectively.

In conclusion, charitable giving is a fundamental aspect of community building and empowerment, particularly within the LGBTQ+ community. By carefully considering your values, researching organizations, and diversifying your giving approach, you can make a significant and lasting impact. Whether through financial contributions, volunteering your time, donating in-kind gifts, or incorporating charitable giving into your estate plan, your generosity contributes to a more inclusive, equitable, and supportive world for all. The act of giving back is not just about supporting others; it's about enriching your own life and making a tangible difference in the lives of others within our community.

Leaving A Legacy Planning for Charitable Donations

Leaving a legacy is a powerful act, and for many in the

LGBTQ+ community, it's a chance to create a lasting impact on the causes and organizations that have shaped their lives. Planned giving, a strategy that involves incorporating charitable donations into your long-term financial plans, offers a unique opportunity to extend your support beyond your lifetime. This allows you to contribute significantly to the organizations you care about, while potentially benefiting from tax advantages.

One of the most common forms of planned giving is a bequest, which is a gift specified in your will. This could involve leaving a specific sum of money, a percentage of your estate, or even a specific asset such as property or stocks to your chosen charity. The simplicity of a bequest makes it an accessible option for many. It's crucial, however, to ensure your will is properly drafted and updated regularly to reflect your current wishes and assets. Consulting with an estate planning attorney is vital, particularly for LGBTQ+ individuals who may face additional legal complexities related to inheritance and recognition of same-sex spouses or partners. An attorney can help navigate the nuances of inheritance laws in your jurisdiction and ensure your wishes are legally sound and effectively executed.

Beyond bequests, charitable remainder trusts (CRTs) offer a more sophisticated approach to planned giving. A CRT is a type of trust where you transfer assets into the trust, and the trust pays you or your beneficiaries a regular income for a set period. Upon the termination of the trust, the remaining assets are distributed to your chosen charity. There are several types of CRTs, each with its own tax implications and benefits. For instance, a Charitable Remainder Unitrust (CRUT) pays a fixed percentage of the trust's assets each year, while a Charitable Remainder Annuity Trust (CRAT) pays a fixed dollar amount annually. The choice between these options depends on factors such as your income needs, the value of your assets, and your desired level of income flexibility. Expert advice from a financial advisor specializing in LGBTQ+ financial planning and an estate planning attorney is crucial for determining which type of CRT best suits your circumstances.

The tax advantages of CRTs are significant. The income you receive from the trust is typically taxed at your ordinary income tax rate, but the growth of the assets within the trust is tax-deferred. This means that you avoid paying capital gains taxes on the appreciation of the assets while they are held within the trust. Furthermore, upon the distribution of the remaining assets to the charity, you or your estate may receive a charitable income tax deduction, further reducing your tax burden. However, the complexities of CRTs require careful planning and consultation with qualified professionals to ensure optimal tax efficiency and alignment with your financial and philanthropic goals. A qualified professional can assist in navigating the intricacies of the tax code and ensuring that your CRT structure is properly established and managed.

Another form of planned giving involves establishing a charitable lead trust (CLT). Unlike a CRT, a CLT pays a predetermined amount to the charity for a set period, after which the remaining assets are distributed to the beneficiaries. This is a useful strategy when you want to make a significant donation to a charity while also providing for your beneficiaries. The tax advantages of a CLT stem from the deduction for the lead payments made to the charity. This strategy can be particularly beneficial for high- net-worth individuals looking to minimize their estate tax liability while significantly contributing to their chosen causes. However, a CLT's complexity requires careful consideration of your overall financial picture and meticulous estate planning.

Don't overlook the simpler, yet impactful, method of naming a charity as a beneficiary on your retirement accounts. Many retirement accounts, such as 401(k)s and IRAs, allow you to designate a beneficiary upon your death. By naming a charity as a beneficiary, you can avoid probate and potentially reduce the overall tax liability on your estate. The funds transfer directly to the charity, minimizing administrative costs and maximizing the amount received by the organization. This is often overlooked, but it offers a straightforward way to support your chosen causes, offering significant tax benefits and streamlining the distribution of assets. However, it's crucial to remember that this can impact your beneficiaries, so it's essential to balance your philanthropic goals with family needs.

Beyond financial instruments, planned giving also extends to the realm of in-kind donations planned for after your passing. This could involve bequeathing artwork, collectibles, or real estate to an organization with the capacity and mission aligned with the assets' value and purpose. This method can offer significant tax benefits as well as a powerful way to leave a unique and lasting legacy tied directly to your interests and passions.

For example, a photographer might leave their extensive collection of prints to a museum or LGBTQ+ arts center. A property owner might bequeath their house to an organization that supports homeless LGBTQ+ youth, allowing the organization to provide stable housing and support. The possibilities are vast, and consulting with the organization beforehand is crucial to ensure your donation aligns with their needs and capacity. They can advise on logistical aspects, such as transportation, valuation, and necessary documentation.

No matter the method chosen – bequests, trusts, or in-kind donations – careful planning is paramount. It's crucial to work with a team of professionals specializing in LGBTQ+ financial planning and estate law to create a personalized plan that addresses your specific needs, values, and goals. An attorney specializing in LGBTQ+ issues can help navigate complex legal landscapes, ensure legal compliance, and protect your interests. A financial advisor can assist in determining the most tax-efficient strategies and managing your assets strategically.

When creating a planned giving strategy, consider the overall financial health of the organization. Research their financial stability and transparency; tools like Charity Navigator and GuideStar can be invaluable in this process. You want to ensure your donation will be utilized effectively and will support the organization's mission in a meaningful way. Don't hesitate to contact organizations directly with questions about their financial practices and how they intend to use your donation.

Beyond the financial aspects, remember that leaving a legacy is also about leaving a positive and lasting social impact. By supporting organizations fighting for LGBTQ+ rights, equality, and social justice, you can contribute to creating a more inclusive and just world for future generations. Your planned giving can amplify the voices and amplify the impact of these organizations, extending your commitment to social change far beyond your lifetime.

Finally, consider the ongoing relationship you might want to develop with the organizations you plan to support. Some organizations welcome opportunities to engage with their major donors or planned giving beneficiaries, offering insight into their programs and work. This connection can be enriching and rewarding, allowing you to see directly how your gift makes a difference.

In summary, planned giving provides a multifaceted approach to charitable contributions, allowing LGBTQ+ individuals to leave a lasting legacy that reflects their values and supports causes they care deeply about. By carefully considering the various options available, seeking professional advice, and thoughtfully selecting organizations, you can create a powerful and lasting impact on the LGBTQ+ community and beyond. This is not merely about financial contributions; it's about shaping a more equitable and just future for generations to come, leaving behind a legacy of compassion, support, and lasting change.

Supporting LGBTQ Youth and Families

Supporting LGBTQ+ youth and families represents a critical area for philanthropic engagement. These young people and their families often face unique challenges, including discrimination, lack of access to resources, and systemic barriers to education, healthcare, and economic stability. Philanthropic contributions can provide vital support networks and opportunities that significantly improve their lives and foster resilience.

Mentorship programs are incredibly valuable for LGBTQ+ youth. These programs pair young people with adult mentors who provide guidance, support, and a safe space for sharing experiences and navigating challenges. Mentors can help young people develop crucial life skills, explore educational and career paths, and build self-confidence. Financial support for these programs is essential, ensuring they can recruit and train mentors, provide resources to mentees, and facilitate meaningful connections. Consider supporting organizations that have robust screening and training processes for mentors, ensuring the safety and well- being of the youth involved. Look for programs with a proven track record of positive outcomes, demonstrating their effectiveness in creating lasting positive impact on the lives of LGBTQ+ youth.

Financial assistance is another critical area where philanthropic contributions can make a significant difference. Many LGBTQ+ youth and families struggle with financial insecurity due to factors such as discrimination in housing and employment, and lack of access to financial resources. This can lead to instability in housing, food insecurity, and an inability to pursue educational opportunities. Donating to organizations that provide financial assistance for housing, food, education, and healthcare can help address these immediate needs and create stability for these families. Support organizations that conduct needs assessments to ensure funding goes to where it is most needed, and transparently share their impact data to illustrate their effectiveness.

Beyond direct financial assistance, philanthropic contributions can also support programs designed to advocate for policy changes at the local, state, and national levels. LGBTQ+ youth and families frequently face discrimination and a lack of adequate legal protections. Advocacy organizations play a vital role in working to change laws and policies that create barriers for these communities. Consider supporting organizations that are actively working to enact inclusive policies related to education, healthcare, housing, and employment. Research groups with a successful history of advocacy, strong leadership, and clear goals. Prioritize groups with demonstrable connections to community stakeholders. Funding litigation efforts to challenge discriminatory laws and policies is also incredibly effective.

Another area deserving of philanthropic support is providing access to culturally competent healthcare services. Many LGBTQ+ individuals face stigma and discrimination in the healthcare system, leading to poorer health outcomes. Supporting organizations that provide healthcare services tailored to the specific needs of LGBTQ+ individuals is essential. This could include supporting organizations that offer mental health services, sexual health services, and gender-affirming care. This might involve funding scholarships for LGBTQ+-affirming healthcare professionals or providing resources for community health centers to develop culturally competent programs. Look for organizations with a strong commitment to diversity, equity, and inclusion within their staff and services.

Supporting LGBTQ+ family structures is equally important. LGBTQ+ families may face additional challenges due to societal norms and legal complexities around adoption, surrogacy, and parental rights. Philanthropic support can help organizations advocate for legal protections for LGBTQ+ families and provide resources to support their needs. This includes supporting organizations that provide legal services, family counseling, and community building opportunities for LGBTQ+ families. Consider organizations actively involved in family planning education, providing LGBTQ+ families with relevant and accessible resources. Supporting organizations focused on the legal rights of LGBTQ+ families is crucial, as navigating legal complexities can be very costly.

Investing in research focused on the unique challenges faced by LGBTQ+ youth and families is critical to developing effective intervention strategies. Funding research can help identify best practices in supporting this community and inform the development of more effective programs. Seek out established academic institutions or non-profit organizations with a proven track record in LGBTQ+ research. Research can help to inform policy, improve program design and enhance the effectiveness of future philanthropic efforts.

Creating safe and inclusive spaces for LGBTQ+ youth and families is a crucial aspect of fostering their well-being. This may involve supporting the creation of community centers, youth groups, or support networks where young people and their families can feel accepted and supported. Support organizations with existing community networks that offer a safe and welcoming environment. Look for organizations with robust community engagement strategies.

Beyond direct financial contributions, consider supporting organizations through volunteer work or in-kind donations. Your time and expertise can be invaluable to the success of these organizations. Volunteering can range from providing administrative support to mentoring youth or directly assisting families. In-kind donations, such as providing office supplies, technology equipment, or professional services, can also make a significant impact on the effectiveness of these organizations. Consider the specific skills and resources you can offer to contribute to an organization's success. Assess the organization's needs and evaluate where your skills and resources can have the greatest impact.

When selecting organizations to support, it's essential to conduct due diligence to ensure they are financially responsible and effectively using their resources. Review their financial statements and look for evidence of transparency and accountability. Explore resources like Charity Navigator and GuideStar, which offer independent evaluations of non-profit organizations. Before making a donation, contact organizations directly to discuss their programs, funding needs, and how your contribution will be used. Understand the organization's mission, its target population and how they plan to achieve their goals. Ensure alignment with your values and priorities to maximize the positive impact.

In conclusion, supporting LGBTQ+ youth and families through philanthropy is an investment in a stronger, more inclusive future. By supporting organizations that provide mentorship, financial assistance, advocacy, healthcare, and safe spaces, we can create lasting positive change in the lives of these individuals and families. Remember, the scope of support is extensive and your contribution, no matter the size, significantly impacts these vulnerable populations. Through careful consideration, research and engagement, you can leave a meaningful legacy of support and create a more equitable world for future generations of LGBTQ+ individuals and their families BUILDING A SUSTAINABLE LEGACY

Building a sustainable legacy requires thoughtful consideration beyond immediate charitable giving. It involves strategically planning how your resources—financial and otherwise—will continue to benefit the LGBTQ+ community long after you are gone. This necessitates a proactive approach encompassing estate planning, charitable trusts, and other mechanisms designed to ensure the enduring impact of your philanthropy.

One powerful tool for building a lasting legacy is the establishment of a charitable remainder trust (CRT). A CRT is a legal entity that allows you to donate assets while retaining a lifetime income stream. Upon your death (or, in some cases, a designated term), the remaining assets are transferred to your chosen LGBTQ+ charity. This structure offers significant tax advantages, reducing your estate tax burden while simultaneously supporting a cause you care deeply about. Different types of CRTs exist – Charitable Remainder Unitrust (CRUT) and Charitable Remainder Annuity Trust (CRAT) – each offering unique income distribution structures. Consulting with a financial advisor and estate planning attorney experienced in LGBTQ+ financial matters is crucial to determine which type best aligns with your financial goals and legacy objectives. They can guide you through the complexities of setting up and managing a CRT, ensuring it effectively achieves both your financial and philanthropic goals. For example, you might consider a CRUT if you anticipate needing a flexible income stream that adjusts with inflation, while a CRAT might be preferred for its predictable, fixed annual payout. This decision requires careful financial planning, taking into account your current income needs, projected expenses, and desired level of charitable giving.

Beyond CRTs, other sophisticated philanthropic vehicles can help build a sustainable legacy. Donor-advised funds (DAFs) allow you to make tax-deductible contributions and invest those funds to grow over time. You maintain control over grant recommendations, distributing funds to your chosen LGBTQ+ charities at your own pace. DAFs offer flexibility, allowing you to strategically allocate your funds across multiple organizations based on their current needs and your evolving philanthropic priorities. This approach lets you maintain a consistent level of support, even if your personal financial circumstances change. This is especially important for long-term support initiatives. For instance, you might choose to support a specific research project over several years, ensuring funding remains available throughout the duration of the project.

Furthermore, establishing a charitable lead trust (CLT) can offer significant tax benefits for high-net-worth individuals. With a CLT, you contribute assets to a trust, which then makes annual payments to a chosen LGBTQ+ charity for a specific period. After that term, the remaining assets are distributed to your beneficiaries. This approach can reduce your estate tax liability while simultaneously providing substantial support to your chosen cause. It's important to understand the complex tax implications of CLTs and seek professional guidance to determine if this structure aligns with your financial situation and philanthropic objectives.

Because of the complex nature of this vehicle, a team approach is always advised. This may include a lawyer specializing in tax law and a financial advisor who understands charitable giving.

Including LGBTQ+ organizations in your will or living trust is another straightforward way to ensure your legacy continues. You can specify the amount or percentage of your estate to be bequeathed to a specific charity or a pool of charities, ensuring continued support for their vital work. This ensures a predictable and reliable flow of funds to the organizations you deeply value. For example, you could designate a specific percentage of your estate to be distributed to organizations supporting LGBTQ+ youth homelessness or healthcare access. These provisions, while seemingly straightforward, require careful drafting to avoid potential legal complications. Consult with an estate planning attorney experienced in LGBTQ+ matters to ensure your wishes are clearly expressed and legally sound. This is critical because the laws governing wills and estates can be complex and vary widely by jurisdiction.

Beyond financial contributions, you can also build a lasting legacy through non-financial means. Mentoring young LGBTQ+ individuals, sharing your expertise and providing guidance, fosters the development of future leaders and advocates. This kind of legacy is immeasurable, passing along invaluable skills and knowledge that will continue to influence and empower the community. Sharing your experiences can provide encouragement and support for those facing unique challenges. Consider developing a mentorship program with a local LGBTQ+ youth organization. This involves investing time and effort, but the lasting impact on the mentees can be immense.

Leaving a legacy also involves advocating for policy changes that directly benefit the LGBTQ+ community. This can involve actively lobbying for legislation, supporting organizations engaged in advocacy efforts, or donating to organizations that focus on policy and legal changes. This might involve supporting litigation efforts challenging discriminatory laws, contributing to organizations working to expand legal protections for LGBTQ+ families, or funding research to identify and address systemic inequalities. This type of legacy leaves a lasting impact that extends far beyond your immediate contributions. It can help to create a more just and equitable society for future generations.

Consider documenting your philanthropic journey and the reasons behind your choices. This can inspire future generations to continue your work and demonstrate the impact of your giving. Create a personal narrative that explains your motivations and shares the stories of the organizations and people you've supported. Your experiences can serve as an inspirational guide for others, encouraging them to engage in meaningful philanthropic activities. This can be a legacy that lives on in writing and can be shared and preserved for future generations to understand the importance of supporting the LGBTQ+ community. This might involve writing a memoir, creating a family archive, or creating a website detailing your philanthropic work and its impact.

Building a sustainable legacy is a deeply personal and multifaceted process. It involves not only financial planning but also engaging with the community, sharing your experiences, and advocating for change. By taking a proactive and strategic approach, you can create a lasting impact on the LGBTQ+ community and ensure your values and commitment continue to benefit future generations. It's a journey that involves careful planning, collaboration with professionals, and a deep commitment to making a positive difference in the lives of others. The true measure of a successful legacy isn't simply the monetary value but the positive influence it has on the community and the lives it touches. The commitment to continuing the work long after your lifetime is the true mark of a lasting legacy. This requires diligent planning, consistent effort and commitment, ensuring that the resources and support will flow to the designated charities even after the benefactor is no longer available.

Impact Investing for Social Change

Impact investing offers a unique avenue for aligning your financial goals with your commitment to social change within the LGBTQ+ community. Unlike traditional philanthropy, which often involves donating assets outright, impact investing seeks to generate both financial returns and positive social or environmental impact. This approach allows you to support LGBTQ+ causes while potentially earning a return on your investment. The crucial aspect lies in identifying investment opportunities aligned with your values and the specific needs of the community

Several investment strategies can facilitate this. For example, you might consider investing in companies with strong LGBTQ+ inclusion policies, demonstrating a commitment to diversity, equity, and inclusion (DEI) within their workforce and operations. Researching companies with a proven track record of supporting LGBTQ+ initiatives, such as employee resource groups, LGBTQ+ focused marketing campaigns, or charitable donations to relevant organizations, is crucial. You might also examine their supplier diversity programs to assess their commitment to supporting LGBTQ+-owned businesses. Don't hesitate to contact companies directly to inquire about their DEI policies and initiatives; many organizations are happy to share this information with potential investors. Transparency and public accountability in this area should be high priorities when selecting investment opportunities.

Beyond individual companies, you can invest in funds specifically designed to generate social impact. These may include community development financial institutions (CDFIs) that provide loans and investments to businesses and organizations in underserved communities, often including those disproportionately impacting the LGBTQ+ population. Some CDFIs focus specifically on lending to LGBTQ+-owned businesses, providing critical access to capital often denied by mainstream financial institutions. Investigate organizations dedicated to supporting LGBTQ+ entrepreneurship, helping to close the funding gap faced by many businesses owned and operated by members of the community. This not only generates potential returns but directly addresses economic inequality within the community. Look for organizations that demonstrate accountability and transparency regarding their investments and social impact metrics.

Investing in social impact bonds (SIBs) presents another opportunity. SIBs are innovative financial instruments that raise capital to fund social programs aimed at addressing specific social issues. If a program succeeds in meeting its pre-defined objectives, investors receive a return on their investment. This model incentivizes effective program design and implementation, ensuring that resources are utilized efficiently to maximize positive outcomes. Research SIBs focused on LGBTQ+ issues, such as initiatives to reduce homelessness among LGBTQ+ youth or improve access to mental healthcare for transgender individuals. These are all critical issues that require innovative solutions and strategi funding to succeed.

Real estate investment can also be aligned with LGBTQ+

causes. Investing in affordable housing developments specifically targeting LGBTQ+ individuals, particularly transgender individuals, senior LGBTQ individuals or LGBTQ youth experiencing homelessness, can generate a financial return while addressing a significant need within the community. Due diligence in this space is essential, including scrutinizing the developer's commitment to fair housing practices and community engagement. Affordable housing initiatives frequently require collaboration among public, private, and non-profit organizations. Understanding how such initiatives are managed and financed is crucial before investing.community. Look for organizations that demonstrate accountability and transparency regarding their investments and social impact metrics.

Investing in social impact bonds (SIBs) presents another opportunity. SIBs are innovative financial instruments that raise capital to fund social programs aimed at addressing specific social issues. If a program succeeds in meeting its pre-defined objectives, investors receive a return on their investment. This model incentivizes effective program design and implementation, ensuring that resources are utilized efficiently to maximize positive outcomes. Research SIBs focused on LGBTQ+ issues, such as initiatives to reduce homelessness among LGBTQ+ youth or improve access to mental healthcare for transgender individuals. These are all critical issues that require innovative solutions and strategic funding to succeed.

Real estate investment can also be aligned with LGBTQ+ causes. Investing in affordable housing developments specifically targeting LGBTQ+ individuals, particularly transgender individuals, senior LGBTQ individuals or LGBTQ youth experiencing homelessness, can generate a financial return while addressing a significant need within the community. Due diligence in this space is essential, including scrutinizing the developer's commitment to fair housing practices and community engagement. Affordable housing initiatives frequently require collaboration among public, private, and non-profit organizations. Understanding how such initiatives are managed and financed is crucial before investing.

By carefully evaluating these aspects, you can minimize risk and maximize the likelihood of achieving both positive financial returns and a significant positive social impact. This detailed due diligence, however, will likely require expert advice. Consult with a financial advisor specializing in impact investing to ensure you understand the investment risks and the potential for achieving social change. Do not underestimate the complexity of such investments; professional assistance can be invaluable.

Remember, impact investing is a long-term commitment. The social and environmental impacts of your investments may not be immediately apparent, so patience and perseverance are essential. However, the potential for creating meaningful and lasting change, aligned with your financial goals, is substantial. By actively engaging in impact investing, you can build a legacy that extends far beyond your financial contributions.

Beyond these specific investment strategies, it's essential to engage directly with the LGBTQ+ community to understand its most pressing needs and identify potential investment opportunities. Attend community events, connect with LGBTQ+ organizations, and seek input from community members to guide your investment decisions. This direct engagement ensures that your investments genuinely address the needs of the community, rather than imposing your own perceptions.

Impact investing offers a dynamic way to advance LGBTQ+ equality while building a portfolio that aligns with your values. The combination of financial returns and social impact offers a powerful tool for shaping a better future for the community. However, navigating this space requires careful research, diligent due diligence, and possibly the expert guidance of a financial professional experienced in impact investing. This comprehensive approach will not only enhance the likelihood of success, but also assure your financial success alongside a substantial contribution to positive social change. The potential to merge personal financial objectives with a commitment to social justice is an exciting opportunity for those who wish to leave a substantial and lasting legacy.

8

RESOURCES AND NEXT STEPS: BUILDING YOUR FINANCIAL FUTURE

Finding LGBTQ Inclusive Financial Professionals

Finding the right financial professional is a crucial step in securing your financial future, especially when navigating the unique financial landscape as a member of the LGBTQ+ community. Traditional financial advice often overlooks the specific challenges and opportunities faced by this demographic. Therefore, seeking out a financial advisor with expertise in LGBTQ+ financial planning is paramount to ensuring your needs are understood and addressed effectively. This requires a more nuanced approach than simply searching for a financial planner.

This search necessitates a proactive and thoughtful strategy. It's not enough to simply rely on online directories or referrals; you need to actively investigate professionals who understand and prioritize the complexities of LGBTQ+ financial life. This involves examining their experience, qualifications, and commitment to the community. Many financial professionals claim LGBTQ+ inclusivity; however, it's essential to delve deeper and verify this claim with concrete evidence. This section will provide you with strategies to effectively identify and connect with LGBTQ+-inclusive financial professionals.

Beyond The Surface: Identifying Expertise in LGBTQ+ Financial Planning

The first step is understanding what constitutes true LGBTQ+ financial expertise. This goes beyond simply displaying a rainbow flag on a website or mentioning diversity in a marketing brochure. True expertise translates to a profound understanding of the multifaceted challenges faced by the LGBTQ+ community, including:

Discrimination and bias: Many financial institutions historically haven't served the LGBTQ+ community effectively, leading to potential discrimination in lending, mortgages, and other financial products. A knowledgeable advisor understands these biases and advocates for fair treatment.

Legal and tax implications of same-sex marriage and partnerships: Navigating the complexities of estate planning, taxation, and inheritance is significantly different for same- sex couples. A financial professional experienced in this area can ensure your assets are protected and distributed according to your wishes, complying with all relevant legal frameworks.

Unique healthcare needs: LGBTQ+ individuals often face higher healthcare costs due to factors such as gender- affirming care or higher rates of mental health concerns. A competent advisor will help incorporate these anticipated costs into your financial planning.

Specific retirement considerations: Retirement planning for LGBTQ+ individuals often involves unique challenges, particularly concerning spousal benefits or accessing appropriate long-term care options. The advisor must understand these nuances and incorporate them effectively into the planning process.

The challenges faced by transgender and non-binary individuals: Transgender and non-binary individuals frequently face specific financial obstacles, including discrimination in employment and housing, as well as higher healthcare costs related to transition-related care. A truly inclusive advisor is sensitive to these unique issues and incorporates them thoughtfully into the financial strategy.

Where To Find LGBT Q+ Inclusive Financial Professionals :

Finding qualified professionals requires a multi-pronged approach, leveraging various resources and networks:

Professional Organizations: Several professional organizations advocate for and support LGBTQ+ financial professionals. Look for organizations that offer certifications, training programs, or networking opportunities focused on LGBTQ+ financial planning. These organizations often maintain directories of their members, providing a reliable resource for finding qualified advisors.

Online Directories and Resources: While general online directories may not always highlight LGBTQ+-specific expertise, some specialized websites and platforms cater to the LGBTQ+ community. Search for these platforms, carefully reviewing profiles to ascertain the advisor's commitment to LGBTQ+ inclusivity. Do not solely rely on self-proclaimed expertise; verify the claims through testimonials, case studies, or references.

Community Organizations: LGBTQ+ community centers, advocacy groups, and non-profit organizations often maintain lists of recommended financial professionals who are actively engaged in supporting the community. These are often excellent resources, leveraging trusted relationships within the community.

Networking: Attending LGBTQ+ community events, conferences, and workshops can be excellent opportunities for networking and meeting financial professionals who understand the community's needs. These settings often provide a less formal, yet highly informative way to connect with professionals and gauge their level of understanding and empathy.

Referrals: Ask for referrals from trusted friends, family members, or other professionals within your network who are members of the LGBTQ+ community or who work closely with the community. Word-of-mouth recommendations often lead to the most reliable and suitable matches.

Beyond Credentials: Assessing Compatibility And Trust

Finding a qualified professional is just the first step. It's essential to assess compatibility and build trust with your chosen financial advisor. This involves:

Initial consultations: Schedule initial consultations with multiple potential advisors to discuss your specific financial goals and concerns. This allows you to assess not only their expertise but also their communication style, empathy, and ability to address your specific needs. Don't hesitate to ask targeted questions about their experience with LGBTQ+ clients and their understanding of the unique challenges you face.

Reviewing their client testimonials: Check their website and online reviews to see what past clients have to say about their experiences. Pay close attention to feedback that specifically addresses the advisor's ability to work with LGBTQ+ clients.

Considering their fees and services: Carefully review their fee structure and ensure it is transparent and aligns with your budget. Clarify the range of services offered and any potential hidden costs.

Evaluating their ethical standards: Ensure that your advisor adheres to high ethical standards, prioritizing client interests and maintaining confidentiality. Ask about their compliance with relevant regulations and their approach to conflict resolution.

Building a strong, trusting relationship with your financial advisor is crucial for long-term success. Choose an advisor who not only possesses the necessary expertise but also demonstrates empathy, understanding, and a genuine commitment to supporting the LGBTQ+ community. This relationship will serve as a cornerstone in securing your financial wellbeing and achieving your financial objectives. Remember, choosing the right financial advisor is an investment in your future; take the time to find the perfect fit. Do not hesitate to continue your search until you find a professional you feel entirely comfortable with and confident in their ability to champion your financial goals.

Additional Resources and Support Organizations

Navigating the complexities of personal finance can feel daunting for anyone, but for members of the LGBTQ+ community, unique challenges often add another layer of difficulty. Discrimination, historical exclusion from mainstream financial services, and the specific financial implications of same-sex marriage and family structures all necessitate a proactive approach to financial planning. While finding the right financial advisor is a crucial first step, access to additional resources and support can significantly enhance your journey towards financial security. This section offers a directory of valuable resources designed to empower you with information, guidance, and a sense of community.

Online Resources And Educational Platforms:

The internet provides a wealth of information, but sorting through the noise to find reliable, LGBTQ+-inclusive resources requires careful consideration. Several websites and platforms offer valuable insights and tools specifically tailored to the financial needs of the LGBTQ+ community. These range from educational articles and webinars to interactive calculators and budgeting tools.

For instance, websites like the National Gay & Lesbian Task Force often feature articles and resources on financial planning, highlighting the unique challenges and opportunities faced by LGBTQ+ individuals. Their resources frequently address issues like estate planning for same-sex couples, navigating healthcare costs, and protecting against discrimination in financial services. Similarly, organizations like Equality Federation offer valuable resources focusing on economic justice and advocating for policies that benefit the LGBTQ+ community. Their website may contain reports, policy briefs, and information on financial literacy programs targeting LGBTQ+ individuals.

Furthermore, many personal finance websites are now proactively including content that specifically addresses the needs of LGBTQ+ individuals. Look for articles or sections dedicated to same-sex marriage and estate planning, transgender financial planning, and discussions of the financial implications of gender-affirming care. Always verify the credibility of sources, looking for evidence of expertise and a clear understanding of LGBTQ+ financial issues. Sites with reputable authors, clear citations, and a history of promoting inclusivity are more likely to provide accurate and helpful information.

Beyond specific LGBTQ+-focused websites, reputable personal finance websites often offer valuable tools and educational materials applicable to everyone, including budgeting apps, investment calculators, and retirement planning guides. These resources, while not specifically targeted at the LGBTQ+ community, can still provide essential tools for managing your finances effectively. However, remember to critically evaluate the information and ensure it accounts for the unique aspects of your financial situation as an LGBTQ+ individual.

Support Organizations and Advocacy Groups:

Navigating the financial world can be overwhelming, and having access to support networks can make a significant difference. Several national and local organizations provide invaluable support, advocacy, and resources specifically for LGBTQ+ individuals.

The Human Rights Campaign (HRC), for example, plays a crucial role in advocating for LGBTQ+ rights and equality, including economic justice. Their website provides valuable resources and information on related legislation and policy changes that might directly affect your financial well-being. Similarly, the National Center for Lesbian Rights (NCLR) offers legal resources and advocacy concerning family law, estate planning, and other legal matters relevant to LGBTQ+ individuals. They often provide information on relevant legal precedents and advocate for legislative changes that protect the financial interests of the LGBTQ+ community.

On a local level, many cities and towns have LGBTQ+ community centers or organizations that provide support services and may offer referrals to financial professionals experienced in working with the LGBTQ+ community. These local organizations often have close ties to the community and can offer valuable guidance on navigating local financial resources and support services. Attending community events organized by these organizations can also be an effective way to network and connect with other LGBTQ+ individuals and potential resources.

It is also crucial to seek out organizations that specialize in specific financial areas, such as housing or healthcare, that may be particularly challenging for LGBTQ+ individuals. Organizations focusing on affordable housing or providing healthcare access resources can be invaluable in addressing specific financial needs. For example, organizations supporting individuals undergoing gender-affirming care may offer information and resources to manage the associated medical costs, potentially connecting you to financial assistance programs.

Publications and Books:

While online resources are invaluable, written publications offer a deeper dive into specific aspects of LGBTQ+ financial planning. Seek out books and articles written by financial professionals with expertise in this area. Many financial publications are now including more LGBTQ+- inclusive content, acknowledging the need for tailored advice for this community. Look for books that explicitly address the unique financial considerations for same-sex couples, transgender individuals, and other members of the LGBTQ+ community.

Furthermore, subscribing to financial newsletters and publications can keep you updated on the latest legislation and regulatory changes affecting LGBTQ+ individuals. Staying informed about changes in tax laws, estate planning regulations, and healthcare policies is crucial for making sound financial decisions. Publications focusing on personal finance and investment strategies often include articles or sections relevant to the LGBTQ+ community, even if not specifically focused on the demographic. Reviewing such articles and publications can contribute to developing a holistic understanding of personal finance.

Networking and Building Community:

Building a support network is vital in navigating the financial landscape. Connecting with other LGBTQ+ individuals facing similar financial challenges can provide invaluable peer support, advice, and encouragement. Attend LGBTQ+ community events, join online forums, and seek out mentorship opportunities. Sharing experiences and learning from others can foster a sense of community and empower you to manage your finances effectively.

Disclaimer: This section provides a directory of resources and is not intended as financial advice. Always consult with a qualified financial professional before making any significant financial decisions. The information provided is for educational purposes only and should not be considered a substitute for professional financial guidance. The specific suitability of any resource depends on your individual financial situation and needs.

Creating Your Personalized Financial Plan

Creating a personalized financial plan is a crucial step towards securing your financial future. This process should be tailored to your specific circumstances, goals, and values, acknowledging the unique aspects of your identity as a member of the LGBTQ+ community. While generic financial advice exists, it's essential to adapt it to address the specific challenges and opportunities that you may encounter. This tailored approach ensures your plan truly reflects your needs and aspirations.

Step 1: Defining Your Financial Goals:

The first step involves clearly defining your short-term and long-term financial goals. These goals can be broadly categorized into several key areas:

Debt Management: This includes strategies for paying off existing debts, such as student loans, credit card debt, or medical bills. Consider the interest rates, payment schedules, and potential strategies like debt consolidation or balance transfers. Prioritize high-interest debts first to minimize overall interest paid.

Emergency Fund: Building a robust emergency fund is paramount. Aim for 3-6 months of living expenses, allowing you to cover unexpected costs like medical emergencies, job loss, or home repairs. This fund provides a crucial safety net, mitigating the financial stress associated with unforeseen circumstances. Consider opening a high-yield savings account to maximize your returns while maintaining easy access to your funds.

Saving and Investing: Determine your savings goals, such as purchasing a home, funding retirement, or investing for future education expenses. Develop a realistic savings plan, allocating a specific amount each month towards your goals. Explore different investment options based on your risk tolerance and time horizon. Consider working with a financial advisor to create a diversified investment portfolio that aligns with your objectives.

Retirement Planning: Retirement planning requires a long-term perspective. Determine your desired retirement lifestyle and calculate the estimated funds needed. Explore various retirement savings vehicles, such as 401(k)s, IRAs, and Roth IRAs, considering the tax implications and potential benefits. Consider factors like potential early retirement, healthcare costs in retirement, and long-term care expenses. Engage with a financial professional to develop a comprehensive retirement plan that accounts for your unique circumstances.

Estate Planning: Estate planning is crucial for protecting your assets and ensuring your wishes are fulfilled. This includes creating a will, establishing a power of attorney, and potentially establishing a trust. For LGBTQ+ individuals, estate planning is particularly vital, ensuring your assets are distributed according to your wishes, even in the absence of legal recognition of certain relationships in some jurisdictions. Consult with an estate planning attorney experienced in working with LGBTQ+ clients to ensure your plan is legally sound and protects your interests.

Healthcare Planning: Healthcare costs can be substantial. Develop a plan to cover potential medical expenses, considering health insurance options, potential deductibles, co-pays, and out-of-pocket maximums. For transgender individuals, planning for gender-affirming care is essential, considering the associated costs and potential insurance coverage. Research resources and financial assistance programs available to help offset these costs.

Homeownership: If homeownership is a goal, develop a plan to save for a down payment, considering mortgage options, interest rates, and closing costs. Explore resources and programs available for LGBTQ+ individuals seeking homeownership, particularly if you have faced discrimination in the housing market.

Step 2: Assessing Your Current Financial Situation:

Once you've established your goals, thoroughly assess your current financial situation. This involves:

Tracking your income and expenses: Maintain a detailed

record of your income and expenses for at least three months. This provides a realistic picture of your cash flow and helps identify areas where you can reduce spending or increase savings. Use budgeting apps or spreadsheets to simplify this process.

Evaluating your assets and debts: List all your assets, including bank accounts, investments, and property. Then list all your debts, including loans, credit cards, and mortgages, noting the outstanding balance and interest rates. This provides a comprehensive overview of your net worth.

Analyzing your credit report: Obtain your credit report from all three major credit bureaus (Equifax, Experian, and TransUnion). Review your credit history for any errors or inaccuracies. A strong credit score is crucial for obtaining loans and credit at favorable rates.

Reviewing your insurance coverage: Assess your health insurance, life insurance, disability insurance, and homeowner's or renter's insurance coverage. Ensure you have adequate coverage to protect yourself and your assets from unforeseen events.

Step 3: Developing Your Personalized Financial Plan:

Based on your goals and current financial situation, develop a personalized financial plan. This plan should outline specific strategies for achieving your goals, including:

Budgeting: Create a realistic budget that aligns with your income and expenses. Allocate funds towards your goals, prioritizing essential expenses and minimizing unnecessary spending.

Debt reduction strategies: Implement strategies for paying off debts, considering debt consolidation or balance transfers.

Savings and investment plans: Establish savings plans for your short-term and long-term goals. Choose appropriate investment vehicles based on your risk tolerance and time horizon.

Retirement planning strategies: Develop a comprehensive retirement plan, contributing consistently to retirement accounts and adjusting your strategy as needed.

Estate planning documents: Create or update your will, power of attorney, and other estate planning documents, consulting with an estate planning attorney.

Healthcare cost management strategies: Explore options to minimize healthcare costs, such as enrolling in a health savings account (HSA) or seeking financial assistance programs.

Step 4: Regularly Review and Adjust Your Plan:

Your financial plan should not be a static document. Regularly review and adjust your plan as your circumstances change. This includes reviewing your budget, investment portfolio, and insurance coverage annually, or even more frequently if significant life events occur (such as marriage, the birth of a child, job changes, or major purchases). Life is dynamic, and your financial plan needs to adapt to these changes.

Step 5: Seek Professional Guidance:

Consider seeking professional guidance from a financial advisor experienced in working with LGBTQ+ individuals. A financial advisor can provide personalized advice, create a comprehensive financial plan tailored to your unique circumstances, and offer support throughout your financial journey. Choose an advisor who understands the specific challenges and opportunities faced by the LGBTQ+ community. This advisor can guide you through the complexities of financial planning, ensuring your plan aligns with your goals and addresses your specific needs. Don't hesitate to seek out a second opinion if needed; finding the right fit is crucial for a successful financial plan.

This step-by-step guide provides a framework for creating your personalized financial plan. Remember, this is a journey, not a destination. Consistent effort, regular review, and proactive adaptation will contribute to your financial well-being and security. By taking control of your financial future, you empower yourself and lay a foundation for a more secure and fulfilling life. Remember to leverage the resources and support networks available to the

LGBTQ+ community to navigate this process successfully.

Monitoring Your Progress And Making Adjustments

Monitoring your progress and making adjustments is an integral part of successful financial planning, particularly for members of the LGBTQ+ community who may face unique financial challenges and opportunities. A static financial plan is ineffective; it's a living document that requires consistent attention and periodic overhauls to remain relevant and effective. Life throws curveballs – job changes, unexpected medical expenses, relationship milestones, or even changes in legislation affecting same-sex couples or transgender individuals – all necessitate reevaluating your financial strategy.

Regular review allows you to track your progress towards your financial goals, identify areas needing improvement, and make necessary adjustments to keep your plan aligned with your evolving needs and circumstances. Think of it as navigating with a map – you wouldn't simply follow the initial route without checking for road closures, detours, or changes in your destination. Similarly, your financial plan needs constant recalibration.

The frequency of review depends on individual circumstances and goals. At a minimum, an annual review is highly recommended. This review should be a comprehensive examination of all aspects of your financial life. This might include:

Reviewing your budget: Analyze your income and expenses over the past year. Are you sticking to your allocated

MONITORING YOUR PROGRESS AND MAKING ADJUSTMENTS

Monitoring your progress and making adjustments is an integral part of successful financial planning, particularly for members of the LGBTQ+ community who may face unique financial challenges and opportunities. A static financial plan is ineffective; it's a living document that requires consistent attention and periodic overhauls to remain relevant and effective. Life throws curveballs – job changes, unexpected medical expenses, relationship milestones, or even changes in legislation affecting same-sex couples or transgender individuals – all necessitate reevaluating your financial strategy.

Regular review allows you to track your progress towards your financial goals, identify areas needing improvement, and make necessary adjustments to keep your plan aligned with your evolving needs and circumstances. Think of it as navigating with a map – you wouldn't simply follow the initial route without checking for road closures, detours, or changes in your destination. Similarly, your financial plan needs constant recalibration.

The frequency of review depends on individual

circumstances and goals. At a minimum, an annual review is highly recommended. This review should be a comprehensive examination of all aspects of your financial life. This might include:

Reviewing your budget: Analyze your income and expenses over the past year. Are you sticking to your allocated original plan, refinancing your loans could significantly reduce the total interest paid over the life of the loan.

Examining your insurance coverage: Assess the adequacy of your health, life, disability, and home/renter's insurance. Have there been significant life changes that warrant a change in coverage, such as marriage, the birth of a child, or a career shift? For instance, increased income may justify a higher life insurance policy or adding long-term care coverage. Changes in health status may necessitate additional health insurance coverage or switching insurance plans. Reviewing your insurance coverage also helps identify potential cost savings without compromising coverage.

Monitoring your retirement savings: Are you on track to meet your retirement goals? If not, what adjustments can be made to increase your contributions or optimize your investment strategy? This could involve increasing your retirement plan contributions, seeking ways to increase your income, or lowering spending in non-essential areas. Adjustments to your retirement portfolio should align with your anticipated retirement date.

Assessing your estate plan: Review your will, power of attorney, and any trusts to ensure they reflect your current wishes and circumstances. Significant life events such as marriage, divorce, the birth of a child, or changes in relationships should prompt a review of your estate plan. Estate planning should also include consideration of any potential tax implications and estate taxes, particularly for those with considerable assets.

Beyond the annual review, you should also trigger a review in response to significant life events. These can include:

Marriage or civil union: This requires reviewing your estate plan, insurance policies, and financial accounts to ensure they reflect your changed status and the legal rights and responsibilities you now share with your partner. Consider joint accounts, beneficiary designations, and the implications of estate taxes as a couple.

Divorce or separation: This necessitates a complete recalculation of your financial situation, including the division of assets, spousal support, child support, and adjustments to your budget, retirement plans and insurance coverage.

Birth or adoption of a child: This profoundly impacts your financial plan, requiring adjustments for childcare expenses, education savings, and potentially adjustments to your insurance coverage.

Job loss or change in employment: This may require a

thorough review of your budget, emergency fund, and long- term financial goals. It might also involve exploring alternative career paths and considering government assistance programs.

Major purchase (home, car, etc.): Large purchases necessitate adjustments to your budget and savings plan.

Regularly reviewing your financial plan and making necessary adjustments isn't just about numbers; it's about proactively managing your financial well-being and adapting to life's inevitable changes. For the LGBTQ+ community, these adjustments may need to incorporate legal considerations concerning same-sex marriage, partnership recognition, transgender healthcare access, and potential discrimination in areas such as housing and employment. Seeking professional advice from a qualified financial advisor with LGBTQ+-specific expertise can be invaluable. They can help navigate the complexities of financial planning and ensure your plan addresses the unique challenges and opportunities you face. Remember, your financial plan is a roadmap; make sure it's always up-to-date and guiding you towards your desired destination. Openly discussing your circumstances with a professional enables more informed and supportive adjustments. Don't hesitate to seek guidance or a second opinion to ensure your financial future remains on the right path. Proactive management of your finances empowers you and provides security for years to come.

Celebrating Milestones and Building Resilience

Celebrating milestones and building resilience are crucial components of a successful financial journey, particularly for members of the LGBTQ+ community who may face unique systemic and interpersonal hurdles. Financial planning isn't just about accumulating wealth; it's about fostering a sense of security and control over your financial life, allowing you to navigate life's transitions with confidence and grace. Acknowledging your accomplishments, no matter how small, is vital in maintaining motivation and celebrating the progress you've made.

This isn't simply about ticking boxes on a checklist; it's about acknowledging the hard work, sacrifices, and often, the sheer courage it takes to navigate the financial landscape, especially within a community that has historically faced discrimination and unequal access to financial resources. Perhaps you've successfully paid off a significant debt, increased your retirement savings, or finally achieved a long- held financial goal, such as buying a home or starting a business. These are significant achievements deserving of recognition and celebration.

Take the time to appreciate these milestones. Reward yourself appropriately—this doesn’t necessarily mean extravagant purchases; it could be something as simple as a quiet night out, a weekend getaway, or indulging in a hobby you enjoy. The key is to acknowledge your efforts and reinforce positive behavior. Celebrating these achievements reinforces the positive momentum and encourages continued progress.

Building resilience is equally important. Life inevitably throws curveballs – unexpected job losses, medical emergencies, relationship changes, or even unforeseen economic downturns. These challenges can be particularly daunting for members of the LGBTQ+ community, who may face additional barriers due to discrimination or lack of social support. Resilience, in this context, is not about avoiding hardship; it's about developing the capacity to bounce back from setbacks, adapt to change, and maintain a positive outlook

Cultivating Resilience Involves Several Key Strategies:

Developing a strong support system: Surrounding yourself with a supportive network of friends, family, and community members is invaluable. This network can provide emotional support, practical assistance, and valuable advice during challenging times. For LGBTQ+ individuals, finding a supportive community is particularly important, as it can counter the isolating effects of discrimination or lack of understanding. Consider joining LGBTQ+ financial support groups or connecting with other LGBTQ+ professionals in your field.

Building an emergency fund: An emergency fund acts as a safety net during unexpected financial crises. Aim to save three to six months' worth of living expenses in a readily accessible account. This cushion provides financial stability during job loss, medical emergencies, or other unforeseen circumstances. The security of having this fund can significantly reduce financial stress and increase your ability to cope with unexpected events. Consider setting up automatic transfers to your emergency fund each month, making saving consistent and effortless.

Developing adaptable financial strategies: Avoid rigidity in your financial planning. Life changes necessitate adjustments to your financial strategies. Be prepared to adapt your budget, investment plan, or debt management approach as needed. This flexibility is key to maintaining financial stability in the face of unexpected challenges. A flexible approach also allows for adjustments based on changing market conditions or personal circumstances. For example, a sudden job loss may require a reevaluation of your budget and a reassessment of your spending priorities.

Practicing self-compassion: Treat yourself with kindness and understanding, especially during difficult times. Avoid self-criticism or negative self-talk. Remember that setbacks are a normal part of life and do not define your worth or potential. Self-compassion involves acknowledging your feelings, accepting your imperfections, and offering yourself the same kindness and understanding you would offer a friend in a similar situation. This is crucial in building resilience and maintaining a positive attitude during challenging circumstances.

Seeking professional help: Don't hesitate to seek professional help when needed. This could include financial advisors, therapists, or other support professionals. Many LGBTQ+ specific organizations offer counseling services and financial literacy programs. These resources can provide valuable guidance, support, and practical assistance in navigating financial challenges.

Building resilience isn't a one-time event; it's an ongoing process that requires continuous effort and self-reflection. It's about cultivating a mindset that allows you to adapt to change, overcome setbacks, and maintain a positive outlook despite adversity.

Financial planning for the LGBTQ+ community often necessitates a deeper level of resilience. Discrimination in employment, housing, and healthcare can create significant financial obstacles. Understanding these challenges and proactively planning for them is crucial. A financial advisor with experience working with the LGBTQ+ community can provide invaluable guidance on navigating these issues and developing strategies to mitigate potential risks.

For instance, the legal landscape surrounding same-sex

marriage and partnerships has evolved significantly, yet inconsistencies remain across jurisdictions. This can impact estate planning, tax implications, and healthcare benefits. A knowledgeable advisor can help you navigate these complexities and ensure your financial plan is legally sound and protects your interests. Similarly, accessing healthcare, particularly for transgender individuals, can present significant financial challenges. Understanding the costs associated with transition-related care and planning for these expenses is vital.

Celebrating milestones and building resilience go hand in hand. Acknowledging your achievements fosters a sense of accomplishment and reinforces positive financial habits. Building resilience equips you to handle life's inevitable curveballs, allowing you to maintain a stable financial footing even during challenging times. By integrating both aspects into your financial planning, you create a holistic approach that promotes both success and sustainability.

Remember, your financial journey is unique to you. Embrace the challenges, celebrate the victories, and remember that you are not alone. Lean on your support network, seek professional guidance when needed, and prioritize self- compassion throughout the process. Your financial well- being is an investment in your overall happiness and well-being. By actively managing your finances and fostering resilience, you are investing in a secure and fulfilling future. This proactive approach enables you to navigate any obstacle with confidence and ultimately achieve a stronger sense of financial independence and peace of mind. The journey may have its ups and downs, but the destination – a secure and prosperous future – is well worth the effort. The celebration of successes, coupled with the development of coping strategies for setbacks, forms a powerful combination for sustained financial health and overall well-being. It's a journey of self-discovery and empowerment, allowing you to take control of your financial destiny and build a future that truly reflects your values and aspirations.

Glossary

Beneficiary: The person or entity designated to receive the proceeds of an insurance policy, retirement account, or will.

Estate Planning: The process of planning for the distribution of assets after death, including creating a will or trust.

LGBTQ+: An acronym representing lesbian, gay, bisexual, transgender, queer, and other gender identities and sexual orientations.

Net Worth: The total value of a person's assets minus their liabilities.

Power of Attorney: A legal document granting another person the authority to make decisions on one's behalf.

Trust: A legal arrangement in which a trustee manages assets for the benefit of a beneficiary.

Will: A legal document outlining how a person's assets will be distributed after their death.

Printable Budget Worksheet

Use this worksheet to plan and track your monthly income and expenses. Fill it out by hand or digitally.

MONTHLY INCOME

Total Monthly Income:

MONTHLY EXPENSES

Total Monthly Expenses:

Difference (Income - Expenses):

Notes:

MONEY AGREEMENT TEMPLATE

Date:

Participants:

1. Shared Financial Values

We agree that the following values will guide our financial decisions:

____

____

2. Income & Contributions

Sources of Income:

• Person A:

• Person B:

Agreed Contribution Toward Shared Expenses:

• Person A: $_______ or __ %

• Person B: $_______ or __ %

Frequency of Contribution (e.g., monthly, bi-weekly):

3. Shared Expenses

We agree to share the following expenses:

4. Individual Expenses

Each person is responsible for their own:

____

____

5. Financial Goals

We agree to work toward the following goals:

____

____

____

6. Communication Agreement

We agree to check in about money:

____

____

• Frequency (e.g., weekly, monthly):

____

• Method (e.g., in-person, video call, shared spreadsheet):

• Safe words or signals for stress check-ins:

____

7. Conflict Resolution

If a disagreement arises, we will:

a. Pause spending decisions related to the issue
b. Discuss in a neutral environment
c. Consider a mediator or financial advisor if needed

8. Agreement Terms

This agreement is:

Ongoing

For a set term:

Review Date:

Signatures

Person A: ______________ Date: ______________

Person B: ______________ Date: ______________

Financial Values Worksheet

Step 1: Reflect on Your Core Values

Review the list below and circle or highlight up to 10 values that resonate with you:

Security, Freedom, Family, Community, Generosity, Health,

Independence, Creativity, Simplicity, Education, Adventure,

Achievement,Justice, Spirituality, Stability, Fun, Connection,

Growth, Activism, Comfort

Step 2: Narrow Down Your Top 5 Values

From the 10 you selected, choose your top 5 financial values that you want to guide your money decisions:

1. ______________________
2. ______________________
3. ______________________
4. ______________________
5. ______________________

Step 3: Connect Values to Money Decisions

For each of your top 5 values, answer the following:

Step 4: Set an Intention

Complete this sentence:

"I want to use my money to support a life that reflects my

values of______________, and______________ ."

Step 5: Action Plan

Choose one financial change you can make this month that reflects your values:

____

____

____

____

____

____

____

____

Debt Tracker Worksheet

Use this worksheet to track your debts, including balances, minimum payments, interest rates, and payment progress.

Debt Overview:

Payment Progress Tracker:

Notes:

www.ingramcontent.com/pod-product-compliance
Lightning Source LLC
LaVergne TN
LVHW050929210926
848482LV00013B/586